HOW OLD IS THE EARTH?

HOW OLD IS THE EARTH?

Dr A. J. Monty White

 EVANGELICAL PRESS

EVANGELICAL PRESS
16/18 High Street, Welwyn, Herts. AL6 9EQ, England.

© Evangelical Press 1985

First published 1985

ISBN 0 85234 198 9

Cover photograph: The Rhum Cuillins from Eigg. Reproduced by kind permission of the Institute of Geological Sciences.

Printed by The Pitman Press, Bath, England.

"Where wast thou when I
laid the foundations of
the earth?"

One of the questions God asked Job

About the Author

Dr A J Monty White was converted to Christianity from atheism in 1964 when he was an undergraduate student at the University College of Wales, Aberystwyth. While he was reading for an honours degree in Chemistry, he studied Geology up to pass degree level. Dr White is a graduate of the University of Wales obtaining his BSc in 1967, and being awarded a PhD in 1970 for his research in the field of Gas Kinetics. He is also a Member of the Royal Society of Chemistry. In 1970 he obtained a Science Research Council Post-doctoral Fellowship and he spent the next two years investigating the optical and electrical properties of organic semi-conductors. Since 1972, Dr White has held various administrative positions in the University of Wales Institute of Science and Technology (UWIST) at Cardiff, where he is now the Academic Registrar.

Contents

Preface

For some time I have thought about writing such a book as this—a short book which looks briefly at the various difficulties with determining the age of the earth. As I travel around giving talks about creation, invariably I am asked about the age of the earth. Is the earth old or is it young? I am aware that although quite a lot of very useful material has been written on this question by creationists, most people are unaware of it. The reason for this is twofold: either the material is too technical or the material is "buried" in a much larger work and so tends to be unknown.

I hope then that in these pages, the reader will get acquainted with the complexity of this subject, ranging as it does from Biblical genealogies to radiometric dating techniques. I also trust that the reader will eventually see that there is, as usual, no conflict between the fact that the Bible teaches that we are living on a young earth and the discoveries of modern science which support this.

My thanks must go once again to my wife for her patience and love, and also for her help in typing the manuscript of this book. I must also thank my Saviour, the Lord God Almighty, who in the beginning created all things, for His patience, His love and His care for me, a sinner saved by grace.

Dr A J Monty White
Cardiff, Wales

General Introduction

How old is the earth? Does it really matter how old it is? How does the answer to this question affect you and your family and even your friends? The answer to this last question is obvious when we consider origins, for there are two irreconcilable views regarding the beginnings of things: evolution and creation. Which one is correct? One thing is certain: if the earth is only a few thousand years old, then evolution cannot be correct, for *evolution needs lots of time*. This factor cannot be overemphasised for we are told that chance natural processes need to operate over eons of time in order to bring about the evolution of life on earth. Darwin was fully aware of the time factor when in *The Origin of Species* he wrote that anyone who "does not admit how incomprehensibly vast have been the past periods of time may at once close this volume" (p.293, Penguin edition, 1968).

Now if we hear of a frog turning *instantaneously* into a handsome prince when kissed by a beautiful princess, then we can safely assume that we are being told a fairy tale. The evolutionist, however, seems to think that given enough time anything will, and can, and even does, happen. For example, we are taught by the theory of evolution that some kind of amphibian (and remember that a frog is an amphibian) has turned into a human being over a period of some 350 million years. This is not regarded as a fairy tale, but as a scientific fact! It seems as if the enormous period of time involved deadens our reasoning so that we believe the unbelievable.

What age then does the evolutionist require the earth to be so that the evolution of life on earth could have occurred? The answer is a staggering four thousand, six hundred million years (4,600,000,000 years). This is almost too much time to imagine. If this time period were represented by *one year*, then *one second* would be equivalent to *146 years*. On such a time scale, Martin Luther, who lived from 1483–1546, would have lived for about half a second some three and a half to three seconds ago; Jesus Christ's earthly ministry would have occurred a mere thirteen and a third seconds ago; and King David, who lived about 1000 BC, would have lived just over twenty seconds ago!

Now if it can be shown that, far from being thousands of millions of years old, the earth is only a few thousand years old, then there will have been no time for evolution to have occurred. And if there has been no time for evolution, then life on earth *cannot* be the product of chance natural processes. Hence the answer to the question "How old is the earth?" is an important one because it will give us the answer, and if not *the* answer, then a very clear indication of the answer, to the question "Creation or evolution?"

The answer to this fundamental question about origins is a very important one and it can have a profound effect upon the way we behave, how we live in society and also upon the very kind of society in which we live. The reason for this is that the theory of evolution maintains that mankind is the product of chance natural processes operating over a long period of time without the intervention of any supernatural agent. This is in complete contrast to the Biblical account of the origin of mankind, which teaches that

God supernaturally created the first human pair a few thousand years ago. Now because evolution is believed by so many scientists, the average person believes that there are scientific reasons for believing in evolution and therefore that there must be scientific reasons for rejecting the Bible and consequently, God.

Many atheists and humanists endeavour to reason in such a fashion. Some argue that if we are just animals, the result of random natural processes, then why should abortion, or even euthanasia, be considered wrong? Putting to death an old sick dog or cat is not considered immoral, so why not an old sick person? Indeed, we can appreciate their arguments, for if we are just animals, and there is no God, then there is no God to sin against. Hence we can see how moral standards become relative and we end up with a "do-as-you-please-so-long-as-no-one-gets-hurt" society. This is the type of society we live in: millions of unborn children are being murdered; thousands of couples are living together unmarried (it *used* to be called "living in sin" — a phrase which accurately conveys the position in the sight of God); hundreds of acts of immorality are being performed; many voices are being raised favouring euthanasia. All this is a direct result of people accepting a theory of origins that eliminates all reference to God.

What I want us to do is to look at the question of the age of the earth and see if the answer we arrive at will throw any light on the fundamental question of evolution or creation. So, how old is the earth?

PART ONE

Biblical Considerations

1.
Introduction

Many people believe that the Bible teaches that the creation took place in 4004 BC and, indeed, this date is often found printed in the margin alongside Genesis chapter one in old Bibles. Although it is generally known that this is Ussher's date for the creation, many do not know who Ussher was, how he obtained this date and how it found its way into the margin of the first page of so many Bibles.

In 1650, James Ussher, Archbishop of Armagh and Primate of Ireland, devised a system of chronology using the Bible that gave the date of the creation as the night preceding 23 October 4004 BC. This date is some seventy-six years earlier than that proposed six years before in 1644 by the distinguished Greek scholar John Lightfoot, who was also the Vice-Chancellor of the University of Cambridge. From textual considerations, he concluded that the creation began at 9 o'clock on the morning of 17 September 3928 BC. Ussher's date of 4004 BC was inserted into the margin alongside Genesis chapter one in the Great (1701) Edition of the English Bible by William Lloyd, Bishop of Winchester. This practice was followed in subsequent editions. In 1900, however, the Cambridge University Press stopped printing this date in their Bibles, followed by the Oxford University Press some ten years later.

On the face of it, calculating the age of the earth

from the Bible is simplicity itself. First the date of Abraham's birth must be determined. Then by using the genealogies in Genesis chapters eleven and five, it should be possible to calculate when Noah and Adam lived, respectively. Finally, a consideration of Genesis chapter one to determine the length of the creation days and also to determine whether there is a chronological gap between Genesis 1 v.1 and 1 v.2 should make it possible to calculate the age of the earth. But it is not as straightforward as this and there are many difficulties, as we shall see.

2.
The Genealogies in Genesis

The *IVP New Bible Dictionary* states on page 7 that "As a result of archaeological discoveries the life and times of Abraham as recorded in Genesis can be shown to accord well with the recent knowledge of the second millennium BC." There is, however, no extra-Biblical method of dating the birth of Abraham to the exact year, because at present Abraham is only known from Biblical sources. Now according to Edwin R Thiele in *The Mysterious Numbers of the Hebrew Kings*, the division of the kingdom of Israel at the death of Solomon occurred in 931 BC. Using the time periods given in 1 Kings 6 v.1 and Exodus 12 v.40, Jacob must have entered Egypt in 1877 BC, and since he was 130 years old at that time (see Genesis 47 v.9), he must have been born in 2007 BC. As Isaac was sixty years old when Jacob was born (Genesis 25 v.26) and Abraham was 100 years old when Isaac was born (Genesis 21 v.5), Abraham (or Abram as he was known at first) must have been born in 2167 BC.

Assuming that the genealogies in Genesis chapters five and eleven are complete and that there is a "father-son" relationship with those named in the genealogies, then, as we can see from table 1, the Flood would have occurred in 2459 BC, 1656 years after the creation and Adam would have been created in 4115 BC. But, are the genealogies in Genesis chapters five and eleven complete? In other

Table 1 Chronology from Adam to Abraham assuming that there are no gaps in the genealogies given in Genesis chapters five and eleven

Name of Patriarch	Year of Birth A.C.	Year of Birth B.C.	Age at Birth of next Patriarch	Year of Death A.C.
Adam	—	4115	130	930
Seth	130	3985	105	1042
Enos (a)	235	3880	90	1140
Cainan (b)	325	3790	70	1235
Mahalaleel	395	3720	65	1290
Jared	460	3655	162	1422
Enoch	622	3493	65	987 (c)
Methuselah	687	3428	187	1656
Lamech	874	3241	182	1651
Noah	1056	3059	502 (d)	2006
Shem	1558 (d)	2561 (d)	100 (d)	2158 (e)
Arphaxad	1658 (d)	2457	35	2096 (e)
Salah (f)	1693	2422	30	2126 (e)
Eber	1723	2392	34	2187 (e)
Peleg	1757	2358	30	1996 (e)
Reu	1787	2328	32	2026 (e)
Serug	1819	2296	30	2049 (e)
Nahor	1849	2266	29	1997 (e)
Terah	1878	2237	70 (g)	2083
Abram	1948	2167	100	2123

Notes A.C. After Creation (of Adam) B.C. Before Christ

(a) Enosh in NIV (b) Kenan in NIV

(c) "By faith Enoch was translated that he should not see death." Hebrews 11 v.5 (AV).

(d) The Flood occurred in 1656 A.C. (when Noah was 600) and Genesis 11 v.10 records that Shem was 100 years old when he begat Arphaxad two years after the Flood.

(e) These dates may not be the year of death.

(f) Shelah in NIV. (g) See text (pp. 25).

words, do they have to be interpreted as a strict chronology? Reasons for believing that they are not complete and that they do not have to be interpreted as a strict chronology have been given by Dr Henry Morris and Professor J C Whitcomb in their well-known book *The Genesis Flood* (pp.474 *ff.*). Let us consider these in a little detail:

(i) *The number of years are not totalled at the end of the genealogies.* This may suggest that the list of names and ages of the patriarchs has not been given us for the purpose of constructing a chronology.

(ii) *The name and years of Cainan do not appear in the Hebrew text but do in the Septuagint.* Cainan appears between Salah and Arphaxad in Luke 3 v.36 and in the Septuagint. This appears to be evidence that not all the postdiluvian patriarchs are listed in the Hebrew text. This indicates that the chronologies are not complete.

(iii) *The genealogies in Genesis chapters five and eleven are symmetrical in form when Cainan is added to the genealogy in Genesis chapter eleven.* In both genealogies, ten patriarchs are listed, with the tenth having three important sons. Even if Cainan were not in the original text, the genealogies would still be symmetrical: Adam to Noah, ten generations; and Shem to Abram, ten generations. This symmetrical arrangement may be an aid to memorisation and may well indicate that it is not necessary to press the numerical data of these chapters into a strict chronology.

(iv) *Information is given concerning each patriarch that is irrelevant to a strict chronology.* For example, in Genesis 5 vvs.6-8, we read in the AV:

"And Seth lived an hundred and five

> years, and begat Enos: And Seth lived
> after he begat Enos eight hundred and
> seven years, and begat sons and daughters:
> And all the days of Seth were nine hundred
> and twelve years: and he died."

Now if the purpose of this genealogy was to provide us with a chronology, all we would need would be:

> "Seth lived an hundred and five years, and
> begat Enos."

The additional facts indicate that the purpose of the genealogy was not to give a simple chronology, but to show how faithfully God guarded the Messianic line.

(v) *The Messianic links were seldom firstborn sons and the age given for the patriarch when he begat the son named in the genealogy is not necessarily the age that patriarch was when that son was born.* This will become clear when we have considered a few examples.

The fact that the Messianic links were seldom firstborn sons becomes obvious when we realise that not one of the Messianic ancestors in Genesis whose background is known in any detail (e.g. Seth, Abram, Isaac, Jacob, Judah and Pharez) was a firstborn son. Furthermore, Genesis 10 v.21 tells us that Japheth was older than Shem, and Genesis 10 v.22 leads us to the conclusion that Arphaxad was Shem's third child.

This leads us onto the second point: namely, that the age given for the patriarch when he begat the son named in the genealogy is not necessarily the age that patriarch was when his son was born. On the face of it, Genesis 5 v.32 informs us that Noah was 500 years old when he begat Shem, Ham and Japheth. We have already seen that

Japheth was older than Shem. In Genesis 11 v.10 we read that Shem was 100 years old when he begat Arphaxad, two years after the Flood. We know that Noah was 600 years old at the time of the Flood (Genesis 7 v.6), hence for Shem to be 100, two years after the Flood, Noah must have been 502 when he was born. Yet Genesis 5 v.32 might have given us the impression that he was only 500.

In Noah's case the difference between the age given in the genealogy and the age he was when Shem was born is only two years, but in the case of Terah and his son, Abram, it amounts to at least sixty years! In Genesis 11 v.26 we read in the AV:

"And Terah lived seventy years, and begat
Abram, Nahor, and Haran."

Taking this verse at face value, we might well conclude that Terah became the father of triplets (Abram, Nahor and Haran) when he was seventy years old. (Remember Isaac became the father of twins when he was sixty years old.) But on further investigation, we discover first of all that Terah was not the father of triplets; secondly, that Abram was *not* the firstborn; and finally, that Terah was at least 130 years old when Abram was born because when Abram was seventy-five years old he left Haran (Genesis 12 v.4) and this happened after his father had died (Acts 7 v.4) at the age of 205 (Genesis 11 v.32). What Genesis 11 v.26 is really telling us is that Terah lived seventy years and begat the first of his three sons, the most important of whom (not because of age but because of the Messianic line) was Abram.

Hence we can see that it is quite possible that

only a few of the patriarchs listed in the genealogies in Genesis chapters five and eleven were firstborn sons. The year of begetting a first son was known in the Old Testament as "the beginning of strength" (see Genesis 49 v.3; Deuteronomy 21 v.17; and Psalm 78 v.51 and 105 v.36). This year was an important one for an Israelite and so it looks as if it is this year, not the year of the birth of the Messianic link, that is given in the genealogies in Genesis chapters five and eleven. This is therefore evidence that these genealogies cannot be interpreted as strict chronology.

(vi) *The term "begat" sometimes refers to ancestral relationships.* Now although in English the term "begat" implies a father-son relationship, this is not necessarily so in Hebrew. For example, in Matthew 1 v.8 we read that "Joram begat Ozias" (AV) implying that Jehoram (or Joram) was the father of Uzziah (i.e. Ozias). But in fact, three generations are omitted, for Jehoram was the father of Ahaziah, who was the father of Joash, who was the father of Amaziah, who was in fact the father of Uzziah.

Also in English, the phrase "the son of" implies a father-son relationship. Again, in Hebrew this is not always so, for in 1 Chronicles 26 v.24 we read that "Shebuel the son of Gershom, the son of Moses, was ruler of the treasures" (AV) in the days of King David. But in this verse, about 400 years of generations are missing between Shebuel and Gershom!

One verse which may have a bearing on the genealogies in Genesis chapters five and eleven is Exodus 6 v.20 (AV):

"And Amram took him Jochebed his

> father's sister to wife; and she bare him
> Aaron and Moses: and the years of the life
> of Amram were an hundred and thirty and
> seven years.''

First of all it is interesting to note that this verse gives the years that Amram lived, striking a close resemblance to the genealogy in Genesis chapter five. Now taking this verse at face value gives the impression that Amram and Jochebed were the father and mother, respectively, of Aaron and Moses. But when we consider this verse in the light of the information given in Numbers 3 vvs. 17-19 and 27-28, we find out that Amram was not the father, but an ancestor of Aaron and Moses and that he lived some 300 years before them. This again is clear evidence that the genealogies in Genesis chapters five and eleven should not be interpreted as strict chronology.

So far, we have considered six reasons for believing that the genealogies in Genesis chapters five and eleven may not be complete and that they do not have to be interpreted as a strict chronology. There are, however, two additional reasons which apply only to the genealogy in Genesis chapter eleven:

(a) *The postdiluvian patriarchs could not have been contemporaries of Abram.* If we accept a strict chronology intepretation of the genealogy in Genesis chapter eleven, then we arrive at some rather incredible and impossible conclusions. In the first place, all the postdiluvian patriarchs, including Noah, would still have been alive when Abram was fifty-five years old. Secondly, three of those who were born before the earth was divided (Shem, Salah and Eber) would have actually outlived Abram (see table 1 for details). Finally, Eber, the father of Peleg, would have not only outlived Abram, but would have lived for two years after Jacob started to work for Laban.

In addition, there is a far more important problem with the statement of Joshua regarding Abram's forefathers being idolators when they lived "long ago...beyond the River" (Joshua 24 vvs.2, 14 and 15 NIV). On a strict chronology interpretation of the genealogy in Genesis chapter 11, we can only come to the inescapable conclusion that all the postdiluvian patriarchs, including Noah and Shem, were still living in Abram's day and that they had fallen into idolatry. Now such a conclusion is false. Hence the premise of interpreting the genealogy in Genesis chapter eleven as a strict chronology must be false.

(b)   *The Bible implies a great antiquity for the Tower of Babel.* Table 1 on page 22 uses a strict chronology interpretation of the genealogies in Genesis chapters five and eleven. From this, we can see that the Tower of Babel episode, which occurred in the lifetime of Peleg, must have occurred between 2358 and 2119 BC, some 200 years before Abram. Now when we turn to the Genesis account of Abram's journeyings, we do not get the impression that the Tower of Babel judgement had occurred only 200 years previously. For example, Abram is not depicted as one of the early pioneers who had left the land of Shinar to go west. The land of Palestine had already been settled and was overflowing with the "Kenites, Kenizzites, Kadmonites, Hittites, Perizzites, Rephaites, Amorites, Canaanites, Girgashites and Jebusites" (Genesis 15 vvs.19-21 NIV), and Egypt was already a mighty empire.

Reading the account of Abram gives the distinct impression that the Tower of Babel judgement had occurred many centuries before the time of Abram.

All the above reasons lead us to the conclusion that the genealogies in Genesis chapters five and eleven may not be complete and that they do not have to be interpreted as a strict chronology. But there are limits to how much these genealogies may be stretched and there are a number of factors that must be borne in mind.

There are twenty names in the patriarchal list from Adam to Abraham. There is a definite father to son relationship between Adam and Seth (Genesis 5 v.3), Lamech and Noah (Genesis 5 vvs.28-30), Noah and Shem (Genesis 9 v.18), Shem and Arphaxad (Genesis 11 v.10) and between Terah and Abraham (Genesis 11 vvs.26-32). Hence there are only fourteen possible generation gaps in the genealogies.

First of all let us consider how many years we would have to put into each of these fourteen possible gaps to date the creation of Adam at about 100,000 BC. The answer is a staggering 6850 years, which is about *twice* as long as the time period from the exodus of the Israelites out of Egypt to the present day. Such long generation gaps seem very unlikely, and would tend to make the genealogies almost meaningless. Now let us calculate the date of the creation of Adam if there were about a thousand years in each of these fourteen possible gaps. (I have deliberately chosen a thousand years because in the New Testament the Lord Jesus Christ was called "the son of David" and there were about a thousand years between David and Jesus.) The date of the creation of Adam that we calculate now is about 18,000 BC.

It is obvious therefore that the genealogies in

Genesis chapters five and eleven cannot be used to calculate the *exact* date on which Adam was created. They cannot, however, be stretched indefinitely, for even dating Adam at 100,000 BC makes the genealogies almost meaningless as we have seen. If we make each possible generation gap about a thousand years then we arrive at a date of 18,000 BC for the creation of Adam. If we do this, then when the genealogy records for example, "And Enoch lived sixty-five years and begat Methuselah," we must interpret it as meaning, "And Enoch lived sixty-five years and begat a son whose descendant 1000 years later was Methuselah."

One thing is abundantly clear, however, and that is that the Bible teaches that Adam was created thousands rather than hundreds of thousands or even millions of years ago.

3.
The Length of the Creation Days

The question of the length of the creation days in Genesis chapter one must now be considered. Are these days literal days or are they longer periods of time? Are they days on which God created, or are they days on which God revealed His creation to Moses, the writer of Genesis? In other words, was Adam created when the world was only six days old or did Adam arrive thousands or even thousands of millions of years after the creation of the earth described in Genesis 1 v.1?

The Hebrew word *yom*, which is translated "day" in Genesis chapter one, can be used to express time in a general sense and is, in fact, translated "time" no less than sixty-five times in the Authorised Version of the Bible. However, it is translated "day" nearly 1200 times and in its plural form *yamim*, it is translated "days" about 700 times. This indicates that the normal meanings of *yom* and *yamim* are "day" and "days", respectively.

This is further strengthened by a consideration of Genesis chapter one. In the first instance, we find the numerical adjectives (first, second, third and so on) being used to indicate that the writer meant a literal day. The passage in Numbers chapter seven can be used for comparison. In the second instance, the Hebrew expression "evening and morning" actually defines the time period of the word *yom*, i.e. a literal

day. The phrase "evenings and mornings" occurs in
Daniel 8 vvs.14 and 26 (NIV) where it clearly means
literal days.

Furthermore, the fact that the days in Genesis
chapter one are literal days is shown conclusively by
considering the fourth commandment in Exodus
chapter twenty. The creation week is used as the basis
of the six work-days and one rest-day and the words
used throughout the text for "day" and "days" are
yom and *yamim*, respectively:

> "Remember the sabbath day *(yom)*, to
> keep it holy. Six days *(yamim)* shalt thou
> labour, and do all thy work: But the
> seventh day *(yom)* is the sabbath of the
> Lord thy God...For in six days *(yamim)*
> the Lord made heaven and earth, the sea,
> and all that in them is, and rested the
> seventh day *(yom):* wherefore the Lord
> blessed the sabbath day *(yom),* and
> hallowed it."

Exodus 20 vvs.8-11 (AV)

Here in this fourth commandment, nothing could be
clearer than that the six creation-days and the one
rest-day of the Lord are identical in duration with the
six work-days and the one rest-day of our seven-day
week that the Lord commands us to have.

In spite of these textual arguments showing that
the days of Genesis chapter one are literal days, some
ask how it is possible to have literal days before the
creation of the sun and moon on the fourth day of
creation. But the fact that the sun was not created
until the fourth day of creation does not make the first
three days of creation indefinite periods of time, for
on the very first day of creation we read that God
created light. The rotating earth would therefore pass
through the same day-night cycle on the first three
days of creation as on the other days.

A fairly common objection made by some to the days in Genesis chapter one being literal days is found in Genesis 2 v.4. Here the word "day", which is a translation of the Hebrew *yom*, means a period of time (the creation week) and some conclude that because "day" *(yom)*, means a period of time here, then it must mean a period of time in Genesis chapter one. This objection is answered by pointing out that in Genesis 2 v.4, it is obvious from the context that the writer is referring to the creation week when he uses the word "day" *(yom)*. Indeed, a parallel construction is found in Numbers 7 v.84 where "day" (again the translation of the Hebrew word *yom*) is used to refer to the twelve previous days referred to in the earlier verses. No-one insists on making the first *day*, second *day* etc. in Numbers chapter seven long periods of time just because of the meaning of the word "day" in Numbers 7 v.84, so why do they in Genesis chapter one? When "day" means a period of time in the Bible, it is always obvious from the context.

Another objection made to the days in Genesis chapter one being literal days is supposedly found in 2 Peter 3 v.8 (AV):

> "But, beloved, be not ignorant of this one thing, that one day is with the Lord as a thousand years, and a thousand years as one day."

Some claim that this verse proves that the days in Genesis chapter one are 1000 year periods! This verse, however, must not be taken out of its context. Peter is writing about those who shall come in the last days (v.3) and who will scoff at the promise of the second coming of the Lord Jesus Christ (v.4). Their philosophy is summed up as "All things continue as they were from the beginning of the creation" (v.4). Now this is the philosophy of the evolutionist—it is called uniformitarianism. Peter, however, reminds his readers that such people are ignorant because God did not use uniformitarian processes in the universal flood which caused "the world that then was" to perish (vvs.5 and 6), neither will the Lord God use uniformitarian processes at His second coming (v.7). What Peter writes in verse 8 is therefore a comment that God can accomplish in one day what appears would take 1000 years to accomplish with uniformitarian processes. It has nothing at all to do with the length of the creation days in Genesis chapter one.

There is an erroneous method of interpreting Genesis chapter one in terms of evolution (and hence concluding that Adam lived a few tens of thousands of years ago and that the earth is thousands of millions of years old) and at the same time retaining the literal meaning of the creation days. This is to maintain that God *revealed* his creation to Moses in six literal days. It is argued by theistic evolutionists advancing this interpretation that Genesis chapter one, rather than being an account of creation, is an account of what God said to Moses. It is argued that the seventh day's rest was instituted for man's sake and that God worked for six days and then rested for one day to show man that he should work for six days and then rest for one day. It has been suggested that although the work God did is not stated in Genesis chapter one, perhaps He made simple models using stones, wood, water etc. to illustrate to Moses the stages of the original creation. This interpretation has been ably propounded by P J Wiseman in his book *Clues to Creation in Genesis.*

As with any evolutionary interpretation of Genesis chapter one, there are contradictions between the Biblical account of creation and the evolutionary account of origins. Adherents to this evolutionary interpretation of Genesis chapter one, however, go to great lengths to reinterpret Genesis chapter one so that some of these contradictions disappear. For example, in a book review on *The Moon: its Creation, Form and Significance* by the creationists Professor J C Whitcomb and Dr Donald B de Young appearing in the November 1979 issue of *Faith & Thought* (the Journal of the Victoria Institute or Philosophical Society of Great Britain), the anonymous reviewer states (p.7), "From the point of view of the language of appearance, it would seem obvious that the sun and moon were 'made' when they first appeared through the mists at an early stage in earth's history." The point at issue is whether or not we are dealing with creation or appearance. Genesis 1 vvs.16 and 17 record that God made the sun and moon; they do not say God *had made* them and then *allowed* them *to appear.*

There are, however, other grammatical problems with this interpretation of Genesis chapter one. In his book *Clues to Creation in Genesis,* P J Wiseman translates Genesis 2 vvs.3-4 as one single sentence (pp.201-202):

> "And God blessed the seventh day and set it apart, for in it he ceased from all his business which God did creatively in reference to making these the histories of the heavens and the earth, in their being created in the day when the Lord God did the earth and the heavens",

whereas the Authorised Version translation has two sentences in these two verses:

> "And God blessed the seventh day, and sanctified it: because that in it he had rested from all his work which God created

and made (*margin:* created to make).
"These are the generations of the heavens
and of the earth when they were created,
in the day that the Lord God made the
earth and the heavens",

as does the New International Version:

"And God blessed the seventh day and
made it holy, because on it he rested from
all the work of creating that he had done.
This is the account of the heavens and the
earth when they were created."

From the AV and NIV translations of verse 3, it is
obvious that God rested from His work of creating
(the translation of the Hebrew word *barah*)—not from
His work of model-making and revealing, which
some theistic evolutionists, including P J Wiseman,
would have us believe.

As with all evolutionary interpretations of Genesis
chapter one, there are also some fundamental
problems in Genesis chapter two for the theistic
evolutionist. Here we read that God "formed man
from the dust of the ground" in verse 7 (NIV) and
that God "had formed out of the ground all the beasts
of the field and all the birds of the air" in verse 19
(NIV). This is not an act of model-making or
revealing, but a definite act of creation. There is no
hint of evolutionary processes being employed here,
and such acts of creation do not fit in with any
evolutionary interpretation of Genesis chapter one.

The idea that God revealed His creation to Moses
in the six days recorded in Genesis chapter one is
therefore erroneous, for it is not supported by
Scripture. It is yet another attempt to make the
Biblical account of origins fit the evolutionary
account. From grammatical and textual arguments,
however, we can see that the days in Genesis chapter

one are to be interpreted as literal days and they are days in which God created. The Bible therefore teaches quite clearly that Adam was created on the sixth day of creation. However, before we conclude that the earth was a mere six days old when this event occurred, let us look at the Gap Theory and investigate whether there is any time interval between the first two verses of Genesis.

4.
The Gap Theory

In 1814, Dr Thomas Chalmers of the University of Edinburgh first proposed the idea of a time gap (and hence the name of the theory) between Genesis 1 v.1 and 1 v.2. The reason for this was *not* theological but to accommodate the views of the geologists of his day, who were demanding vast periods of time, whilst at the same time attempting to maintain a literal interpretation of the Genesis account of the creation. The Gap Theory was further elaborated in 1876 by George H Pember in his book *Earth's Earliest Ages* and it has been enormously popularised by the footnotes found to it in the *Scofield Reference Bible* which was first published in 1917.

The Gap Theory proposes that the original earth created in Genesis 1 v.1 was populated with plants and animals (including "pre-Adamic men"!) but because of the fall of Lucifer (i.e. Satan) this original creation was destroyed by God by a universal cataclysmic flood. At the same time, the earth was supposedly plunged into darkness and thus *became* "without form and void" as recorded in Genesis 1 v.2. The vast ages of evolutionary geological time are supposed to have occurred during this time interval so that the fossils found in the earth's crust are supposedly relics of the originally perfect world which was supposedly destroyed *before* the six literal days of *re*-creation recorded in Genesis 1 vvs.3-31.

The Gap Theory gets support because, on the face of it, it offers rather impressive Biblical support for a position that does not radically challenge the evolutionary geological time-table. But on closer inspection, as pointed out by Professor J C Whitcomb in his book *The Early Earth*, it "comprises the unity and completeness of the creation account, the original perfection of the world, the genetic continuity of fossil and living forms, the totality of Adam's dominion, and the uniqueness of both the Edenic Curse and the global catastrophism of Noah's Flood" (p.131). In fact, the differences between the Gap Theory and the Scriptural teaching of a comparatively recent creation in six literal days are quite profound:

  (i) The Gap Theory compromises the teaching of Adam's dominion over God's creation, for in Genesis 1 v.26, we read that God said concerning mankind, "And let them rule over the fish of the sea and the birds of the air, over the livestock, over all the earth, and over all the creatures that move along the ground" (NIV). If the Gap Theory interpretation is correct, then Adam (the first man) would have been placed on a world that had just been destroyed by God and so he would have been literally walking upon the graveyard of billions of creatures over which he would never have exercised his rule.

 (ii) The Gap Theory assumes that carnivorous and omnivorous animals were living and dying not only millions of years before Adam, but even before the fall of Satan! This is contrary to the clear teaching of Scripture that the "groaning and travailing in pain" of the animal kingdom is a result of the Edenic curse, which came *after* Adam's fall.

(iii)   The Gap Theory must redefine the "very good" of Genesis 1 v.31 where we read that "God saw all that he had made, and it was very good" (NIV). If the Gap Theory is correct, then this "very good" world was a graveyard of billions of creatures and was already the domain of Satan who is described in 2 Corinthians 4 v.4 as "the God of this world" (AV).

(iv)   According to the Gap Theory, all the plants and animals of the original world were destroyed and fossilised and so could have no genetic relationship to the living things of the present world. Yet the majority of the fossils appear to be identical in form to modern types. Also there are so-called "living fossils" found on the earth today and these are identical to those found fossilised e.g. the *Coelocanth* fish, the *Ginkgo*, *Araucaria* and *Cycas* conifers and the horsetail plant, *Equisetum*. More importantly, however, some adherents to the Gap Theory interpretation of Genesis chapter one place human fossils into the time gap, and so they are forced to the conclusion that pre-Adamic men existed but that they did not possess an eternal soul.

(v)   If the Gap Theory were correct, then we would be left with no clear word from God concerning the original perfect world—*nothing* concerning the order of events in its creation; *nothing* of the arrangement of its features; *nothing* of its history (which could have constituted over 99.9% of the earth's history). The Christian would be expected to look to the evolutionist to provide the answers to his curiosity about such matters.

(vi)   Finally, the Gap Theory tacitly assumes that Noah's Flood (to which Moses devotes three entire chapters in Genesis) was comparatively insignificant from the standpoint of its geological and hydrodynamic effects, since all the major fossil-bearing formations would have been laid down by the supposed flood of Genesis 1 v.2.

When we turn to grammatical and linguistic considerations of the Gap Theory, we find that it cannot be supported. Weston Fields in his book *Unformed and Unfilled* has considered the meanings of the Hebrew words *asah* (to make) and *barah* (to create) and the relationships between these two words. He concludes that the meaning of these words is such that it "allows no time for a gap between Genesis 1:1 and 1:2; it allows for no gap *before* Genesis 1; and it requires *recent creation*". (p.74). After examining the grammar of Genesis 1 v.2, Weston Fields concludes that "The clauses of which it is composed are a description of the action of the main verb (namely, the action of creating the heaven and the earth in Genesis 1:1), *not a chronologically sequential development after 1:1.*" (p.86). The "was" of Genesis 1 v.2 is shown to be the traditional and *only* legitimate translation of the Hebrew *hayeta,* thus negating one of the forceful arguments of the Gap Theory. Weston Fields also examines the phrase which is translated "without form and void" and he shows "that neither lexical definitions, nor contextual usages require that we view Genesis 1:2 as a scene of judgement — an evil state created by the fall of angels." (p.129). He concludes that the Hebrew words *tohu* and *bohu* are being used to describe "something unfinished, and confused, but not necessarily evil!" (p.129).

The book *Unformed and Unfilled* is a fine rebuttal of what is probably the "standard work" on the Gap Theory, *Without Form and Void* by Arthur C Custance. As well as the arguments considered in the last paragraph, Weston Fields also considers all the other arguments about the Gap Theory, such as the darkness, 2 Corinthians 4 v.6, Hebrews 11 v.3, sin, fossils and pre-Adamic man, Lucifer's flood and *katabole* (the Hebrew word which is translated "foundation" in the phrase "from the foundation of the world" which occurs in Matthew 25 v.34; Luke 11 v.50; John 17 v.24; Ephesians 1 v.4; Hebrews 4 v.3 and 9 v.26; 1 Peter 1 v.20; and Revelation 13 v.8 and 17 v.8. Proponents of the Gap Theory insist that this word should be translated "disruption".). In each case, it is shown that the arguments of the gap theorists are "sterile, based on theological biases, and extraordinarily strained" (p.146).

The Gap Theory then is a compromise...a modern theory only formulated in the last couple of centuries in an attempt to harmonise the Biblical account of the creation with evolution. We have seen, however, that the Gap Theory does not rest upon the impregnable rock of Holy Scripture. We are forced therefore to the conclusion that there is no time gap between the first two verses of Genesis—Adam was therefore created when the earth was a mere six days old.

5.
Superficial Appearance of Age

Before we conclude our Biblical considerations regarding the age of the earth, there is one further factor that we must consider. This is the fact that when God created, He did so giving things a superficial appearance of age. This factor is very relevant to the whole question of the age of the earth and we shall return to it again in our general conclusion.

It is important to understand *exactly* what the phrase "superficial appearance of age" means and also to realise its significance. In order to do this, it will be useful for us first of all to consider one or two of the miracles that our Lord Jesus Christ performed during His earthly ministry. This will then give us a much clearer understanding of the phrase "superficial appearance of age".

The account of Jesus Christ's *first* miracle is found in chapter two of the Gospel according to John. Jesus was at a wedding in Cana of Galilee and at the reception He turned about 600 litres of water into wine. Now the difference between water and wine is enormous—you only have to taste the two to confirm this! Water is a relatively simple substance with the chemical formula H_2O (as every schoolboy should know). Wine, on the other hand, is a very complex solution containing a great number of complex organic compounds (alcohols, esters, fatty acids, pigments etc.). You could argue that in nature the water found in the soil is changed into wine by the natural processes involved in the formation of grapes and their fermentation to produce wine. The water in the soil is absorbed by the root of the vine and is eventually turned into grape juice in the grape as it ripens. The juice is squeezed out of the grape and is fermented by yeast until the sugar in it has been converted into ethyl alcohol. Other alcohols, acids and esters are also produced. After fermentation has ceased, the wine has to mature for several months before it is palatable. The chemistry of maturation is quite complex. Hence the natural process of transforming water into wine is complex and takes several months and sometimes years.

Jesus Christ, however, accomplished this transformation *immediately*. The wine, only minutes old, had a superficial appearance of age, for it appeared to have an age of several months, if not years. As John 2 v.10 shows, the people at the wedding feast thought it was ordinary (though good) wine which the host had kept until then, and that it was the end product of the fermentation and maturation of the fruit of the vine. The wedding guests could not tell the difference between this *created* wine and ordinary naturally-produced wine!

The notion of superficial appearance of age is again illustrated by considering the miracle of the feeding of the five thousand. Professor J C Whitcomb puts it like this in his book *The Early Earth* (p.30):

> "One evening on a mountainside near the Sea of Galilee, five thousand men and their families ate loaves and fishes that were created with an appearance of age. Here were tens of thousands of barley loaves composed of grains that had neither been

> harvested from fields nor baked in ovens!
> And here were at least ten thousand fishes
> that had never hatched from eggs or been
> caught in nets or been dried in the sun!"

We can see the same idea illustrated again by considering the story of the blind man healed by the Lord Jesus Christ, as recorded in John 9 vvs.1-7. Here was a man who had been born blind—he presumably had congenital blindness. Yet after being healed, he appeared never to have been blind. In other words, his (recently healed) eyes could be said to have had a superficial appearance of age.

This concept is further illustrated by considering many of the miracles that the Lord Jesus Christ performed in His earthly ministry: e.g. the healing of the man who had a withered hand (Matthew 12 vvs.10-13); the healing of the woman who had been bent double for eighteen years (Luke 13 vvs.11-13); the healing of the deaf and dumb (Mark 7 vvs.32-35 and 9 vvs.17-27); and the raising of the dead (Matthew 9 vvs.18-25, Mark 5 vvs.22-42, Luke 7 vvs.12-15 and John 11 vvs.1-44). These miracles all serve to illustrate and elucidate the significance of the concept of "superficial appearance of age".

With this concept fixed firmly in our minds, let us now consider the creation as recorded in Genesis chapter one. This, too, had a superficial appearance of age. For example, when God commanded the earth to bring forth fruit trees, He did not create seeds first and then wait for a number of years for them to grow to maturity. No! God's command was fulfilled by the act of the creation of full-grown fruit trees bearing fruit. Similarly, all the other plant life which appeared on the third day of creation was created mature. The fish that swarmed in the sea and the fowl that flew in the air were also created fully grown on

the fifth creation day. The animals which appeared
on the sixth day of creation were also created fully
adult—so, too, were Adam and his wife, Eve. Such
acts of creation are in complete harmony with God's
later works in the Holy Land at the time of Christ.

Everything, then, was created with a superficial
appearance of age. Professor J C Whitcomb uses the
following arguments to further emphasise this point
in his book *The Early Earth* on pp. 33 and 36:

> "It is really quite impossible to escape the
> conclusion that if God created living
> things *after their kind*, as the first chapter of
> Genesis states ten different times, He must
> have created them with a superficial
> appearance of age. And the Scriptures
> inform us that God began the cycle of life
> with adult organisms rather than with
> embryonic forms. Both Old and New
> Testaments concur in the supernatural
> creation of Adam and Eve, as adults. And
> must not this have been true also of all the
> kinds of animals? How could such
> creatures have existed as mere fertilised
> eggs outside of the mother's womb? And
> how could infant mammals have survived
> without a mother's care? God would have
> had to intervene directly and continually
> to care for them. Therefore, unless we
> appeal to an endless supplying of miracles,
> the direct creation of *adult* organisms
> remains as the only logical interpretation
> of the Genesis account of the creation of
> living things *after their kind*."

Hence we can see clearly that the Bible teaches that
God created a mature creation that had a superficial
appearance of age. And this not only applied to the

living world but also to inorganic things. If we could be transported back in time to when the earth was only eight days old, then we would see such features as mountains, valleys, sandy beaches and rocky sea shores which naturally often take thousands of years to form. This concept of superficial appearance of age is an important one, and it is one to which we shall have to return after we have looked at the scientific considerations regarding the age of the earth.

6.
Conclusion

In the introduction to this part on the Biblical considerations of the question of the age of the earth, we saw that, on the face of it, calculating the age of the earth from the Bible is simplicity itself. However, when we considered the question in detail, we ran into problems. We saw, for example, that the genealogies in Genesis chapters five and eleven may not be complete and that they do not have to be interpreted as a strict chronology, hence they cannot be used to calculate the exact date on which Adam was created. We did see, however, that the genealogies cannot be stretched indefinitely, for even dating Adam at 100,000 BC makes these genealogies almost meaningless.

When we turned our attention to the length and the meaning of the days in Genesis chapter one, we saw that from grammatical and textual arguments, these days are to be interpreted as literal days and they are days in which God created. We also saw that there is no evidence from the Scriptures for there being any chronological gap between Genesis 1 v.1 and 1 v.2.

From these considerations, we have to conclude that although we do not know the exact date on which Adam was created, we do know that he was created on the sixth day of creation. From Biblical considerations we are almost certain that this event occurred within the last 100,000 years. We have also considered the nature, with respect to superficial appearance of age, of God's initial creation and we have concluded that God created a mature creation. This concept of superficial appearance of age is an important one and it is one to which we will have to return after we have looked at the scientific considerations regarding the age of the earth.

PART TWO

Scientific Considerations

7.
Introduction

Before we pose the question "How old is the earth?" and try to answer it from purely scientific considerations, let me ask you, the reader, "How old are you?" You know the answer to this question because you have a written record—a birth certificate—which tells you when you were born. This is the *proof* of your age. Generally speaking, we know *when* certain events occurred in the past from written records. In fact, such written records are the only reliable method of knowing when an event occurred—even then you must be sure that the writer was telling the truth.

But how can you date something about which there is no written record? This is the problem that we are faced with when we try to determine how old the earth is without using the written record contained in the early chapters of Genesis. How is this problem overcome? What methods can be used to determine the age of the earth? Are these methods reliable? Can we ever *know* how old the earth really is?

In the second part of this book, I want us to look at the various scientific methods that have been used to determine the age of the earth. We shall consider the various radiometric dating methods that give ages of thousands of millions of years for the rocks on the earth. We shall consider the assumptions on which the radiometric dating methods are based, and see if the vast ages which are obtained using these methods are reliable or not. Finally, we shall look at what scientific evidence there is for believing that the age of the earth should be measured in thousands rather than thousands of millions of years.

8.
Dating Methods

Some of the earliest attempts to determine the age of the earth were made during the last century. One of these was to calculate how long it would take for various salts in the ocean to build up to their present concentrations based on present-day rates of accumulation. That is, the amount of any given chemical in the ocean was divided by the annual increment of that chemical via river inflow. Such a simple age determination of the earth assumes that the particular chemical was not present in the ocean to begin with and that the rate of inflow of that particular chemical has always been the same. It also assumes that the particular chemical is not being precipitated out anywhere or being recycled in any way.

Now since there are many chemicals in the ocean, many different calculations can be made. Interestingly, they all give different answers, as can be seen in table 2, where the times taken for twelve different elements to accumulate in the ocean from river inflow are listed. The reason that different times are obtained is that an unknown amount of each element was present in the ocean to start with. Also, in some cases, some mechanism for recycling *may* exist to return a proportion of that element back to the continents for transportation to the ocean again.

We can see, therefore, that such a relatively

Table 2   Time Taken for Various Elements to
Accumulate in the Ocean from River
Inflow

Chemical Element	Years to Accumulate
Sodium	260,000,000
Magnesium	45,000,000
Silicon	8,000
Potassium	11,000,000
Copper	50,000
Gold	560,000
Silver	2,100,000
Mercury	42,000
Lead	2,000
Tin	100,000
Nickel	18,000
Uranium	500,000

Taken from *Chemical Oceanography*, Edited by J P
Riley and G Skirrow (Academic Press, London,
1965) volume 1, p. 164.

"simple" method will not give us the age of the earth. The real problem is: how do you date a rock? For example, when were the rock strata upon which your home is built laid down? How can we really know the answer to such a question if no-one was there to observe these rock strata being deposited and to record it for posterity? These are the questions to which we shall address ourselves in the rest of this chapter.

In the book *Scientific Creationism,* no less than nine types of information are listed that are *not* used to date rocks (pp. 132 *ff*). It will be worth considering these in turn so that we can remove certain popular misconceptions about how rocks are dated. We shall consider each of the points in turn, following closely the arguments and often the wording:

(i) *Rocks are not dated by their appearance.* Supposed old rocks do not necessarily look old; neither do supposed young rocks look young. That is, rocks which are dated as very old may actually be quite loose and unconsolidated, while rocks that are supposedly very young may be dense and compact.

(ii) *Rocks are not dated by their petrological character.* Rocks of all types—shales, granites, limestones, conglomerates, sandstones, etc.— may be found in all "ages".

(iii) *Rocks are not dated by their mineralogical contents.* There is no relation between the minerals or metallic ores that might be found in a rock and its supposed age.

(iv) *Rocks are not dated by their structural features.* There is not necessarily any kind of physical break (unconformity) between any one "age" and its succeeding "age". Faults and folds and other structural features bear no relationship to the chronology of the rocks.

(v) *Rocks are not dated by their adjacent rocks.* Rocks of any "age" may rest vertically on top of those of any other "age". The very "oldest" rocks may occur directly beneath those of any subsequent "age".

(vi) *Rocks are not dated by vertical superposition.* Often "old" rocks are found resting vertically, sometimes in perfect conformity, on top of "younger" rocks. Normally, sedimentary rocks are formed with the earliest sediments deposited on the bottom, and successively younger sediments deposited in ascending order, so that vertical position ought to provide at least a local relative chronology. The many cases of "inverted order", however, make this rule apparently an unreliable guide.

(vii) *Rocks are not dated radiometrically.* Many people believe that the age of rocks is determined from the study of the radio-active elements they contain, but this is not so. Dr Morris points out (p.133) that "The obvious proof that this is not the way it is done is the fact that the geological column and approximate ages of all the fossil-bearing strata were all worked out long before anyone ever heard or thought about radioactive dating." He goes on to say that "There are so many sources of possible error or misinterpretation in radiometric dating that most such dates are discarded and never used at all, notably whenever they disagree with the previously agreed-on dates." (We shall look at radiometric dating in great detail in the next chapter.)

(viii) *Rocks are not dated by any physical characteristics at all.*

There is nothing whatever in the physical appearance or content of a rock that is used to determine its "age".

(ix) *Rocks are not dated by their total fossil contents.* A great many fossils are remains of organisms that still live in the modern world. This makes them useless as geochronological indices.

How, then, are rocks dated? How does the geochronologist (that is the name given to the scientist who determines the age of rocks) decide that such and such a rock belongs to a certain geological age or period and is therefore so many years old? The answer is by its *index fossil.* J E Ransom in his book *Fossils in America* (Harper and Row, New York, 1964) explains (p.43) this as follows:

> "In each sedimentary stratum certain fossils seem to be characteristically abundant: these fossils are known as index fossils. If in a strange formation an index fossil is found, it is easy to date that particular layer of rock and to correlate it with other exposures in distant regions containing the same species."

Now, *index fossils* are the remains of organisms, usually marine invertebrates, that are assumed to have been widespread geographically but with a rather limited duration chronologically. Hence their presence in any rock is supposed to date that rock unambiguously. But the question that now needs answering is: how does the geochronologist *know* how old the index fossil is? The answer to this question is *evolution.* But there is tautology or circular reasoning here:

> The rocks are dated by index fossils, the age of which is determined by evolution.
> On the other hand, the proof of evolution is the age of the rocks in which the fossils are found.

Hence the basis of dating rocks is evolution and the only proof of evolution is the ages of the rocks in which the fossils are found. The main evidence for evolution is therefore the assumption of evolution! Hence the fossils really cannot provide a satisfactory method for dating rocks. Hence there is no real *proof* from the sedimentary rocks that the vast evolutionary time scale is valid.

It is argued by the evolutionary scientist, however, that the great thicknesses and varieties of sedimentary rocks *require* long ages for their deposition and lithification. Indeed, we are told this so often that we hardly ever question it. Yet the very existence of fossils in the sedimentary rocks establishes the fact of the rapid formation of fossil-bearing sedimentary rocks. Dead organisms do not become fossilised during slow rates of sedimentation deposition because the forces of erosion, weathering, bacterial decay or some other disintegration process would destroy the remains of the organism long before it would be able to be fossilised.

Turning our attention to the formation of sedimentary rocks, we see that sands only become sandstones under very unusual conditions: they need a cementing agent. And if such an agent is present, then the sandstone would form quickly, just as hard mortar forms quickly from sand when Portland cement and water are added. Similarly, silts and clays require a cementation agent in order to become shales, siltstones or mudstones. When this agent is present, this transformation is rapid. This same type of reasoning can be applied to the formation of other sedimentary rocks, including conglomerates. It has also been proposed by Dr Henry Morris that limestones could be formed rapidly by "massive precipitation from solution in chemical-rich waters, when conditions of pH, temperature, etc., changed suddenly" (*Scientific Creationism*, p.104).

Beds of common salt, gypsum, anhydrite and other such salts are called evaporites—a name which suggests or implies that the beds were formed by long periods of evaporation from inland salt-water seas or lakes. There is, however, another mechanism for the formation of evaporites and this is by rapid precipitation, not by long periods of evaporation. (See Omer B Roup, "Brine Mixing: An Additional Mechanism for Formation of Basin Evaporites", *Bulletin, American Association of Petroleum Geologists*, volume 54, p.2258, December 1970). Furthermore, the Russian geophysicist Sozansky has shown that evaporite deposits could be, in most cases, the product of juvenile origin through tectonic movements (V I Sozansky, "Origin of Salt Deposits in Deep-Water Basins of Atlantic Ocean", *Bulletin, American Association of Petroleum Geologists*, volume 57, p.590, March 1973).

Evolutionary scientists also cite other evidences of supposed long periods of formation. These include the existence of fossil coral reefs, desert sandstone deposits, glacial deposits, oil and coal. In each case, as we shall see, it can be shown that the evidence is such that these formations could have been formed relatively quickly:

Fossil coral reefs: Such fossil reefs are different from modern coral reefs, as pointed out by H Blatt, G Middleton and R Murray in their book *Origin of Sedimentary Rocks* (Prentice-Hall, 1972) on p.410:

> "Closer inspection of many of these ancient carbonate 'reefs' reveals that they are composed largely of carbonate mud with the larger skeletal particles 'floating'

> within the mud matrix. Conclusive
> evidence for a rigid organic framework
> does not exist in most of the ancient
> carbonate mounds."

Indeed, the creationist geologist Stuart Nevins has shown that the El Capitan Permian "reef complex" in West Texas is not a true reef at all, but largely an "allochthonous" (transported into place from elsewhere) deposit of fossil-bearing lithified lime mud.

Desert sandstone deposits: There is considerable controversy among orthodox evolutionary geologists whether such deposits are water-laid rather than wind-laid. The sharp cross-bedding noted in such deposits can be produced by violent water action. The sandstones of the Colorado Plateau contain interbedded mudstones and siltstones, with some of the best known fossil dinosaur graveyards in North America. Concerning this, Dr Morris points out in *Science, Scripture and the Young Earth* that "It is extremely unlikely that dinosaurs could have lived in a desert environment or that the fossil beds could have been formed in any way except by flooding" (p.14). This indicates a rather rapid deposition and subsequent lithification.

Glacial Deposits: There are no real problems about the Pleistocene glacial deposits, but there are about the much more equivocal evidence of earlier ice-ages, for example, the so-called Permian ice-age and the ones in the Pre-Cambrian. First of all, it should be noted that striated bedrock and conglomerates which are often quoted as being indicators of glaciation may be produced by causes other than glaciers—an obvious example is floods. For example, fifty-five thousand million cubic metres of coarse sedimentary rock in Australia, formerly interpreted as a 'tillite' originally deposited in an ancient glacial period, have been shown to have been formed by subaqueous mud flows. (J F Lindsay "Carboniferous Subaqueous Mass-movement in the Manning-Macleay Basin, Kempsey, New South Wales", *Journal of Sedimentary Petrology*, volume 36, pp.719-732, 1966).

Oil and Coal: Long ages need not be required to convert organic material into oil, as has been shown by the recent laboratory manufacture of oil from garbage! (See for example Larry L Anderson, "Oil Made From Garbage", *Science Digest* volume 74, p.77, July 1973). Also, Professor Melvin Cook has concluded that "The long times generally attributed in the past to the coal cycle are unfounded" (*Prehistory and Earth Models*, p.214). He also cites evidence of mine timbers coalified to the anthracite level in a mine which had been sealed up for ten years (p.217).

Not only are we told that rocks take a long time to form, but we are also told so do land features such as sandy beaches, raised beaches, caves, coves etc. Yet there is evidence that such geomorphological features can be produced in a matter of months! In 1963, the new island of Surtsey appeared 70km south of Iceland. The following year, the Icelandic geophysicist Sigurdur Thorarinsson visited the island and gave the following description of its geomorphological features:

> "Only a few months have sufficed for a landscape to be created which is so varied and mature that it is almost beyond belief...Here we see wide sandy beaches and precipitous crags lashed by breakers of the sea. There are gravel banks and lagoons, impressive cliffs resembling the White Cliffs on the English Channel. There are hollows, glens, and soft

undulating land. There are fractures and faulted cliffs, channels and rock debris. There are boulders worn by the surf, some of which are almost round, and further out there is a sandy beach where you can walk at low tide without getting wet."

Surtsey (Almenna, Reykjavik, 1964)

Such features had been formed in months, not years or even hundreds of years.

In this chapter, then, we have considered how rocks are dated, and we have seen that of the many characteristics that you may think might be used to date rocks, the one that is used is the index fossil. We have seen that the age of the index fossil is based on its supposed evolution and so a rock is dated by assuming evolution. We have seen that there is evidence for the rapid formation of sedimentary rocks and that there is an eye-witness account of geomorphological features, which are thought to take hundreds or even hundreds of thousands of years to form, occurring within a matter of months. The only reason for believing that the earth is old seems to be evolution!

9.
Radiometric Dating

One method favoured by the geochronologist that is used to determine the ages of rocks is that of radiometric dating. This method relies on the fact that certain isotopes of certain elements are radioactive. These isotopes, which are called radio-isotopes, are unstable and decay into other elements—these are often referred to as "daughter" elements. For example, the isotope of the element uranium, which is called uranium-238, decays into the isotope of lead, which is called lead-206. Radio-carbon, an isotope of carbon called carbon-14, decays into nitrogen-14, whereas potassium-40 decays *either* into argon-40 *or* calcium-40. (See table 3 for details.) Sometimes the decay process is a simple one-step decay process, as in the case of radiocarbon; other times, it is more complex with several intermediate steps, such as with uranium-238, which decays to lead-206 via no less than fourteen steps—see table 4.

The principle of radiometric dating is straight-forward. When a molten rock cools and solidifies (e.g. a lava flow), then any radio-isotope which is trapped in the rock will begin to decay into its daughter element(s). By measuring the amount of parent and daughter element(s) in the rock and by knowing the rate at which the parent element decays into its daughter element(s), then the date at which the rock formed (i.e. when it solidified) can be determined by

Table 3   Some Common Radio-Isotope Decays
which are used as the basis of Radiometric Dating Methods

(i) **Radiocarbon Dating**

$$C_6^{14} \rightarrow N_7^{14} + e_{-1}^0$$

Radiocarbon gives nitrogen plus electron

(ii) **Potassium-Argon Dating**

(a) 90% of the potassium-40 decays by beta
emission:

$$K_{19}^{40} \rightarrow Ca_{20}^{40} + \beta_{-1}^0$$

potassium-40 gives calcium-40 plus beta particle

(b) 10% of the potassium-40 is converted to argon-40
by electron capture:

$$K_{19}^{40} + e_{-1}^0 \rightarrow Ar_{18}^{40} + \gamma$$

potassium-40 plus electron gives argon-40 plus gamma
emission

(iii) **Rubidium-Strontium Dating**

$$Rb_{37}^{87} \rightarrow Sr_{38}^{87} + \beta_{-1}^0$$

rubidium-87 gives strontium-87 plus beta particle

Table 3 continued

(iv) **Uranium-Thorium-Lead Dating**

(a) **Uranium-238 – Lead-206 Dating**: This decay proceeds step-wise as shown in table 4. Eight *alpha* and six *beta* particles are emitted.

(b) **Uranium-235 – Lead-207 Dating**: This decay also proceeds step-wise with the overall emission of seven *alpha* and four *beta* particles.

(c) **Thorium-232 – Lead-208 Dating**: Again there are many steps as the thorium-232 decays to lead-208 and six *alpha* and four *beta* particles are emitted.

---

the geochronologist. There are, however, several assumptions that are made by the geochronologist, and these have quite an effect on the accuracy of such age determinations using radiometric dating methods, as we shall see.

In radiometric dating, it is *always* assumed that the *rate* of decay of the parent element into its daughter element(s) is a *constant*. In fact, pupils studying physics and chemistry in schools are taught that nothing can change the rate of decay of a radio-isotope. But this is not so! It has been shown, for instance, that the rate of decay of the radio-isotope beryllium-7 changes as the pressure changes. This pressure dependence was reported in 1973 in *Science* (volume 181, number 4104, pp.1164-65). Two years earlier, in 1971, it was reported at the 161st National Meeting of the

Table 4 The Uranium-238 – Lead-206 Decay

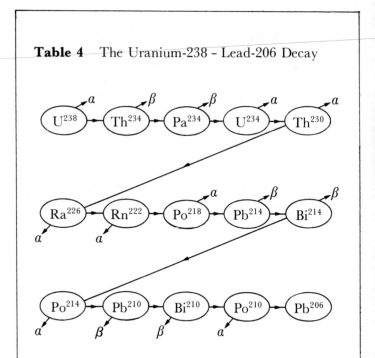

Taken from *Critique of Radiometric Dating* by H S Slusher (Institute for Creation Research, San Diego, 1973) page 11.

American Chemical Society held at Los Angeles that the amount of radiation (i.e. a measure of the amount of decay) emitted from molecular monolayers (i.e. single layers of atoms) of carbon with carbon-14 added, was not the same as that calculated assuming a constant radiocarbon decay rate. There is also evidence that the decay rates of uranium into lead vary with time. This evidence comes from the work of Professor Robert Gentry at the Oak Ridge National Laboratory and his studies of pleochroic haloes— these are dark rings which appear around minute uranium-containing mineral inclusions in, for example, mica crystals when the crystals are viewed in thin rock section under a microscope.

Some radio-isotope decay rates cannot be measured directly and so the measured rate is often dependent upon other radio-isotope decay rates. For example, as shown in (ii) of table 3, potassium-40 decays in one of two ways. It is, in fact, the decay shown in (ii)(b) which is used in potassium-argon dating. The rate of decay of this electron capture process is impossible to measure directly, and it is determined by calculating the best value which gives potassium-argon dates that agree with dates obtained by the uranium-thorium-lead method of dating on the same rock sample. In other words, the accuracy of the measurement is dependent upon knowing accurately the rate of another decay rate, and assuming that that rate is also a constant, and we know that there are doubts about this assumption in the case of uranium isotope decay rates, as we have seen.

The *second* assumption concerns how much of the parent and daughter element(s) were present in the rock when the rock formed (or, more correctly, solidified). You may think that it is assumed that there was no daughter present, but this is often not the case. For example, the age of the earth is determined by measuring the amounts of uranium and lead on the earth and assuming the composition (i.e. the amounts of uranium and lead) present in the earth when it formed (see for example *Geological Time* by Professor J F Kirkaldy, pp.70-71). It cannot be overemphasised that *no* rock on the earth has ever been dated as being 4,600 million years old.

In the potassium-argon method of dating, the amount of argon-40 present in the rock when the rock formed (i.e. when it solidified) is often estimated. This is done by assuming that some of the argon-40 present in the rock came from the atmosphere. The amount of argon-36 in the rock sample is measured and then by *assuming* that the ratio of argon-36 to argon-40 in the atmosphere *today* has remained unchanged for hundreds of millions of years, the amount of argon-40 present in the rock initially is calculated. We can see here that such a calculation is based on an assumption and we have no way of telling if this assumption is correct.

With rubidium-strontium dating, it is impossible to distinguish between the strontium-87 in the rock which has been formed from the rubidium-87, and the strontium-87 which was in the rock when the rock formed. The geochronologist estimates the amount of strontium-87 that was present when the rock formed by measuring the amount of strontium-87 in the calcium plagioclase crystals in the same rock and then it is assumed that this was the concentration of strontium-87 in the potassium-bearing crystals in the rock when it formed. In practice, the geochronologist measures the total amount of rubidium-87, strontium-86 and strontium-87 in each mineral in the rock mass and then draws a graph on which the ratio strontium-87/strontium-86 is plotted against the ratio rubidium-87/strontium-86. This graph is called an isochron diagram and if all goes well (and many times it does not), then the date on which the rock solidified and crystalised can be calculated from the slope of the isochron which has been plotted. The intersection on the vertical axis gives the initial ratio of strontium-87/strontium-86. But the problem is that there is no way of knowing if this ratio was a constant throughout the whole rock, and if it was not, then the isochron is meaningless.

The *third* assumption that is made in radiometric dating is that the system has remained "closed" since the rock formed i.e. that no parent or daughter element(s) were added to or taken out of the rock from the time of its solidification. This assumption is one about which it is simply not possible to know if it is correct or not for any rock sample, the age of which the geochronologist is attempting to determine. For example, with the potassium-argon dating method, potassium can be easily leached out of the rock by the rainwater percolating through the rock because potassium salts are so soluble in water. Furthermore, the argon, produced by the decay of the potassium, can easily diffuse through the rock and the rate of diffusion will not only depend upon the type of rock, but also upon its depth in the earth's crust, because pressure will affect this rate. Both of these factors will cause a false age to be obtained for a rock where this leaching and/or diffusion has occurred.

"The proof of the pudding is in the eating," so the old proverb goes. The proof of radiometric dating methods is therefore in their accuracy. Usually, only one radiometric method of dating can be used to determine the age of a rock, so very often no check can be made, unless of course, the age of the rock is

really *known*. One example of this is the age obtained
by potassium-argon dating for 200-year-old lavas on
the ocean bottom on a submarine extension off the
east rift zone of Kilauea. The Hawaiian Institute of
Geophysics reported ages up to twenty-two million
years! (*Science* volume 162, p.265, 11 October 1968.)
Similar modern rocks formed in 1801 near Hualalei,
Hawaii were found to give potassium-argon ages
ranging from 160 million to 3,000 million years.
(*Journal of Geophysical Research* volume 73, p.4606, 15
July 1968.) The point here is that the ages of these
lava flows were known from historical sources. If we
had to rely solely on potassium-argon dating, then we
would be lost, not knowing the correct age of these
lavas.

This sometimes happens and very often the age is
guessed at. For example, a study on Hawaiian basalts
has obtained seven ages ranging from zero years to
3,340,000 years. (*American Journal of Science* volume
262, p.154, February 1964.) The authors felt justified
in recording the "age" of these basalts as 250,000
years. They did this by the use of statistical reasoning!

Another way of testing the accuracy of radiometric
dating is to compare the ages obtained by different
methods for the *same* rock. Here again inaccuracies
abound. For example, a report was published in
Nature Physical Science (volume 232, pp.60-61, 19 July
1971) which gave the following ages for the *same*
basalt rock found in Nigeria:

Conventional Geology:	Upper Tertiary i.e. about 2-26 million years
Fission Tracks:	Less than 30 million years
Potassium-argon:	95 million years
Uranium-helium:	750 million years

Very often the *same* method of dating will often give
different ages for different rocks which are supposed

to be the same age. A research paper published in 1976 in *Science* (volume 193, pp.1086-1094) listed twenty-two examples of rocks of "Tertiary Age" (sixty-five million years old or less according to the geologist) that have been dated using the rubidium-strontium method of dating. These are reproduced in table 5, where it can be seen that the ages range from seventy to 3,340 million years. The authors of the paper attempt to explain the errors(!) as being due to varying degrees of inheritance of source area radiometric age characteristics for material which has been transported by plutonic or volcanic processes.

The internal consistency of the uranium-238—lead-206 dating method has been checked by the creationist S P Clementson and reported in the *Creation Research Society Quarterly* (volume 7, pp.137-141, December 1970). By assuming constant half-lives for all the steps in the uranium-238—lead-206 decay (see table 4) and by assuming that no lead-206 was present at the time of the crystalisation of a rock, Clementson computed the differing amounts of the daughter elements (i.e. uranium-234, thorium-230, radium-226, radon-222 etc.) that would form and from these the various ratios of daughter to parent elements (i.e. U^{234}/U^{238}, Pb^{206}/U^{238} and so on) that would be present in the rock after various periods of time had elapsed. Hence by measuring the various ratios of daughter to parent elements in a rock, it should be possible to determine the rock's age. Using research figures published about recent volcanic rocks from Faial Azores, Tristan da Cunha and Vesuvius, Clementson showed that the ages obtained using these ratios of daughter to parent elements range from 100 million to 10,500 million years. Yet in fact these volcanic rocks are only a few hundred years old!

Table 5   Rubidium-Strontium radiometric ages
for selected volcanic material.

Location	Association	Apparent Age (Million Years)
United States	Absaroka volcanic field: andesites	3340 ± 1540
United States	Western Grand Canyon: hawaiites	1300 ± 290
United States	Western Grand Canyon: alkali basalt series	1100 ± 240
United States	Colorado Plateau: basalts	960 ± 240
United States	Snake River Plain: King Hill basalts	940 ± 210
Spain	Jumilla, alkalic complex: jumillites	780 ± 390
United States	Snake River Plain: Craters of the Moon basalts	620 ± 60
United States	Absaroka volcanic field: shoshonites	470 ± 50
Peru	Arequipa volcanics: andesites, dacites	440 ± 70
Uganda	Napak alkalic complex: nephelinites, ijolites	380 ± 340
Peru	Barroso volcanics: andesites, dacites	310 ± 50
United States	Columbia River group: basalts, andesites, dacites	290 ± 80
United States	Basin and Range: basalts	200 ± 70
United States	Northwest Great Basin: basalts, andesites	190 ± 80
United States	Navajo alkalic province: trachybasalts, lamprophyres	170 ± 110
United States	Leucite Hills: lamproites, orendites	150 ± 80
New Zealand	East arc: North Island: basalts, andesites	110 ± 20
United States	Cascades, Glacier Peak: basalt, andesites	110 ± 90
United States	Cascades, Mt Lassen: basalts, andesites, dacites	100 ± 50
Uganda	Budeda alkalic complex: ijolite series	80 ± 50
United States	Bearpaw Mountains alkalic complex: syenites etc.	80 ± 40
Uganda	Torror alkalic complex: phonolites, nephelinites, etc.	70 ± 5

Data taken from table 1 of C Brooks, D E James and S
R Hart "Ancient lithosphere: its role in young
continental volcanism", *Science*, volume 193, pp.
1086-1094 (1976).

Occasionally, dates obtained from two or more radiometric methods do happen to agree, and this is interpreted as proof of the accuracy of radiometric dating. In view of the rarity of such concordances, it may well be that such are fortuitous coincidences. Most published dates are from discordant data, but even more significantly, most discordant data are never published at all. It is often simply assumed that discordant dates indicate open systems, which are therefore unsuitable for dating purposes, and so they can be ignored.

We can see then that radiometric dating is based on the assumption that the decay rate of a radio-isotope is constant, even though there is experimental evidence that in one or two cases this is not so; on assumptions regarding the initial conditions which are not always known; and on the assumption that the system is closed, even though very often we do not know if this is so. Because of the problems with these assumptions, we should expect radiometric dating to be unreliable. We have seen that in general, this is so; different radiometric dating methods giving different ages for the same rock, though, occasionally, concordant ages are obtained. These odd occasions when ages agree should not be used as proof that radiometric dating is accurate and that the earth is therefore 4,600 million years old. In fact, one or two radiometric dating methods can be used to show that the age of the earth should be measured in thousands of years rather than thousands of millions of years, as we shall see.

10.
Evidence for a Young Earth

In this chapter, I want us to consider some of the scientific evidence which indicates that we are living on a young earth. Even though such evidence exists, unfortunately it is not often given the publicity it deserves. The evidence comes from a variety of scientific disciplines, including radiometric dating, as hinted at in the last paragraph of the previous chapter. Before we look at the evidence from this particular method of dating, let us look at some surprising data obtained from a study of the solar system.

The solar system is made up of the sun and the nine major planets that revolve around it. The nine planets are Mercury, Venus, Earth, Mars, Jupiter, Saturn, Uranus, Neptune and Pluto. Most of these planets have moons revolving around them. In addition to these nine major planets and their moons there are the asteroids: some of these are "rocks" just a few miles in diameter; others are minor planets a few hundred miles in diameter. The asteroids are found in the main between the orbits of Mars and Jupiter. Meteors (small particles of rock and dust) and comets are the other components of the solar system. Now although its age is usually quoted as 4,600 million years, there is evidence, as we shall see, that the age of the solar system and hence the earth should be measured in thousands rather than thousands of millions of years.

The first piece of evidence that the solar system is relatively young is the fact that short-period comets are still found in the solar system. The head of a comet is about 100km across and it is made up of particles of ice, dust and debris (it can be thought of as a dirty snowball!). The tail of a comet is the result of particles being blown off the comet's icy head by high-energy emission from the sun—this is why the tail always points away from the sun. (The comet becomes visible when sunlight is reflected off the ice and dust particles in the tail.) The result of this process is that a comet is continually undergoing disintegration as it travels in its orbit around the sun. Eventually, a comet will disintegrate to the point where it ceases to exist.

The time it takes for a comet to make one full orbit of the sun is known as its period. So-called short-period comets orbit the sun in less than 150 years, in contrast to long-period comets that may take as long as a million years! Now because of the continual disintegration of comets, the British astronomer R A Littleton has concluded that "Probably no short-period comet can survive more than about 10,000 years". (*Mysteries of the Solar System*, Clarendon Press, Oxford, 1968, p.110).

Since short-period comets and the planets, together with the asteroids, all orbit the sun as part of one system, astronomers logically conclude that all these parts are of the same age. Because short-period comets are short-lived i.e. about 10,000 years, and because there are short-period comets in the solar system (e.g. Halley's comet which has a period of about seventy-six years) then the only logical conclusion is that the solar system, and hence the earth, is less than 10,000 years old.

This conclusion is not accepted by evolutionary astronomers, who cannot accept such a young age for the solar system. To circumnavigate such an unacceptable (to them, at least) conclusion, astronomers have suggested that short-period (i.e. short-lived) comets are supplied to the solar system so that at any time, there are always short-period comets orbiting the sun as part of the solar system. Some of the short-period comet supply ideas are strange, to say the least, and others border on the ridiculous. One such bizarre idea is that these comets were formed by volcanoes on Jupiter, in spite of the facts that the comets' orbits make this impossible and there is no known way for a comet to be shot upwards fast enough to escape from Jupiter's gravitational pull and remain intact.

Most comet supply ideas contain so many flaws that only one has gained any popularity—that of Oort's. He has suggested that there is a vast cloud or shell of comets around the solar system and that, every so often, one gets drawn into the solar system by the gravitational interaction with a passing star. This shell is supposed to contain about 200 thousand million comets and is supposed to be 30,000 to 100,000 times further from the sun than is the earth and is, conveniently, beyond the limits of visible detection. The British astronomer R A Lyttleton has demolished Oort's theory in a critique entitled "The Non-existence of the Oort Cometary Shell" *(Astrophysics and Space Science*, volume 31, pp.385-401, 1974). Despite this, however, the idea remains popular because of the fact that short-period comet break-up times contradict the evolutionary belief in vast ages.

The second piece of evidence from the solar system indicating that we are living on a young earth is from a study of the amounts of cosmic dust particles that enter the earth's atmosphere from space and then gradually settle onto the earth's surface. The best measurements of this influx of micrometeoric dust have been performed by Hans Patterson ("Cosmic Spherules and Meteoric Dust", *Scientific American*, volume 202, p.123, February 1960). He obtained a figure of fourteen million tons per annum for this influx. If the earth has been in existence for 4,600 million years, then 6.5×10^{16} tons of dust would have settled onto the earth during this time. Dr Henry Morris has shown on page 152 of his book *Scientific Creationism* that if we assume that the density of compacted dust is 140 lbs per cubic foot (i.e. 2.3 gms/cm^3), then this corresponds to a volume of 10^{18} cubic feet. Now since the surface area of the earth is 5.5 x 10^{15} square feet, then this means that about 182 feet (i.e. about 56 metres) of this micrometeoric dust should have accumulated on the earth!

There is, however, no sign of such a large accumulation of this dust on the earth (nor, interestingly, on the moon!). The usual explanation given for its absence on the earth is that erosional and mixing processes are continually removing it from the earth's surface. Now the composition of this dust is quite distinctive in that it contains about 2.5% nickel, which is a rare element in the earth's crust and oceans. The amount of nickel falling onto the earth's surface every year is therefore 2.5% of 14 million tons, i.e. 350 thousand tons. Now it is estimated that the oceans contain about 3,300 million tons of nickel. If we assume that all the micrometeoric dust that settles on the earth's land surfaces is washed into the oceans by the rivers, then there is only just over 9,000 years' worth of nickel in the oceans. In other words, the oceans' nickel content could have accumulated from the influx of micrometeoric dust in just over 9,000 years. This assumes, of course, that the rate of influx is fairly constant and that nickel is not precipitating out on the ocean bottom. There is no evidence that nickel is being precipitated out on the ocean bottom. In fact, if it did precipitate out, and the influx of micrometeoric dust had remained the same as now for 4,600 million years, then you would expect to find about 960 lbs (i.e. about 430 kg) of nickel on every square foot of ocean bed!

Now there are two things that should be noted about the influx of micrometeoric dust. The first is that although Patterson's experiments gave a figure of fourteen million tons per annum for the influx of micrometeoric dust, he was "inclined to find five million tons per year plausible" (p. 132). Using this value of influx in the above calculations gives the age of the earth as just over 26,000 years — still considerably less than 4,600 million years so often quoted by the evolutionist.

The second thing to note is that in 1972, in a review article "Interplanetary Objects in Review: Statistics of their Masses and Dynamics" in *Icarus* (volume 17, pp. 1-48, 1972), J S Dohnanyi gave the influx of micrometeoric dust as twenty-two thousand tons per annum. This influx is the one which is quoted by anti-creationists in an attempt to discredit scientific arguments for a young earth (e.g. G Brent Dalrymple "Radiometric Dating and the Age of the Earth: A Reply to Scientific Creationism" given at a symposium *The Creationist Attack on Science* presented by the American Society of Biological Chemists at the sixty-sixth Annual Meeting of the Federation of American Societies for Experimental Biology at New

Orleans, Louisiana on 19 April 1982 and published in
Federation Proceedings volume 42, number 13, October
1983, pp. 3033-3038). If, however, Dohnanyi's value
for the influx of micrometeoric dust is used in the
calculations above, then the age of the earth is
calculated to be about six million years — still far
short (4,594 million years short, in fact) of the 4,600
million years age for the earth that evolutionists such
as Brent Dalrymple believe! One thing, however, is
abundantly clear and that is that the influx of
micrometoric dust indicates a young earth and
Patterson's measurements of this influx indicate an
age of just a few thousand years.

What is even more strange, however, is that we find
this dust in interplanetary space at all. The
micrometeoric dust particles are so small that they
are affected by the pressure of sunlight. This so-called
Poynting–Robertson effect tends to slow these
particles down so that they gradually spiral in
towards the sun. In his book *The Earth, the Stars and the
Bible,* Paul Steidl, who holds a Master of Science
degree in astronomy, has calculated that because of
the Poynting-Robertson effect, "within 10,000 years
all such dust should be completely gone" (p.60). This
assumes that the dust is not being replenished.
However, we have already seen that when comets
near the sun, then some of their material is lost. This
amount is very small, for Paul Steidl also points out
on page 60 of his book that "the amount of matter in
2000 cubic miles of Halley's comet's tail is less than
the amount of matter in one cubic inch of air at the
earth's surface". In other words, the amount of
material being dispersed in the solar system from the
disintegration of comets is not enough to replenish the
amount falling into the sun. This has been estimated
to be eight tons per second by W K Hartmann on

page 170 of his book *Moons and Planets* (Belmont: Wandsworth, 1973).

Furthermore, in their very detailed study of the Poynting-Robertson effect and the extinction of interplanetary dust, Slusher and Duursma conclude:

> "None of the mechanisms for resupplying the dust complex in the solar system seem adequate for maintaining the dust complex against the forces of extinction for any time remotely approaching evolutionary guesses on the age of the solar system. The short-period comets which have been suggested as a major source of resupply for the dust complex certainly do not appear as a source for very long since the evidence points to their early demise around ten thousand years at the most after their origin.
>
> If the major portion of the dust and particulate matter presently in the interplanetary medium originated at the same time as the solar system, as many astronomers hold, then the time for spiralling into the sun, because of the Poynting-Robertson effect, puts an upper limit on the age of the solar system vastly less than the evolutionary estimates of its age. In less than two billion years any matter would be swept into the sun that is less than 182.88 cm (6 ft) in diameter inside earth's orbit; less than 7.62 cm (3 in) in diameter inside Jupiter's orbit; and less than 0.225 cm (0.1 in) inside Neptune's orbit. Considering the fact that dust particles much smaller than those are still

around in great abundance in the
interplanetary medium there would seem
to be a maximum to the age of the solar
system on the order of just several
thousand years."
                    (Taken from *The Age of the Solar
                                    System* pp. 84-85)

Having shown that there is scientific evidence from
the solar system that the earth is less than 10,000 years
old, let us look at evidence from other scientific
disciplines that also suggests that the earth is only a
few thousand years old. First, I want us to consider
the evidence for a young earth that comes from
radiometric dating. It may come as a surprise that the
very method of radiometric dating which is quoted to
prove that the earth is 4,600 million years old is the
very same method which indicates that the earth is
less than 12,000 years old, as we shall see.

As the radio-isotopes of uranium and thorium
decay, they emit *alpha* particles, which are helium-4
nuclei. As these *alpha* particles slow down, they pick
up electrons to form helium-4 atoms. Now this
helium-4 migrates fairly quickly through the earth's
crust into the atmosphere. It is possible to calculate
the amount of helium-4 being produced by the decay
of uranium and thorium, knowing how much of these
elements are in the earth's crust. In his book *Nuclear
Geology* (John Wiley, New York, 1954), Henry Faul
cites evidence to show that the efflux of helium-4 into
the atmosphere is over 3×10^{11} gms per year. As the
atmosphere contains 3.5×10^{15} gms of helium-4, the
time it has taken for this amount of helium-4 to be
produced in the atmosphere can be calculated by
dividing this amount by the rate at which helium-4 is
being formed. This time is just over 11,000 years.

Some argue that you cannot do such a simple calculation because the helium-4 is passing through the atmosphere and being lost to space and that the present rate of loss through the atmosphere to space balances the rate of efflux from the earth's crust. But this equilibrium idea is an assumption and there is no evidence that helium-4 either does, or can, escape from the atmosphere in significant amounts. On the contrary, in his article "Where is the Earth's Radiogenic Helium?" published in *Nature* (volume 179, p.213, 26 January 1957), Professor Melvin Cook has shown that there is a strong possibility that helium-4 is actually *entering* the atmosphere in significant amounts (3×10^9 gms per year) from cosmic rays. Hence the uranium-thorium-helium method of determining the age of the earth gives a figure of about 11,000 years. This figure is obtained on the assumption that no helium-4 was present in the earth's atmosphere to begin with.

From a detailed study of the amount of carbon-14 in the biosphere, it is possible to show that the earth's atmosphere is not very old. In the upper atmosphere, nitrogen is transmuted into the isotope of carbon called carbon-14 (also called radiocarbon). This transmutation of nitrogen into radiocarbon is due to its being bombarded by neutrons, which in turn are generated as a result of the bombardment of the upper atmosphere by cosmic radiation. Carbon-14 is radioactive decaying into nitrogen.

The newly formed carbon-14 in the atmosphere combines with oxygen in the air to form carbon dioxide. This carbon dioxide diffuses through the atmosphere and is assimilated by plants during photosynthesis and also by animals which ultimately live on plants. When an organism dies, it is unable to take up further carbon-14 and the amount which is already present in the organism diminishes due to radioactive decay. Because of this it should be possible to determine when an organism has died if you know the rate of decay and the initial concentration of carbon-14 in the organism. This is the basic theory behind radiocarbon dating. (For a detailed criticism of radiocarbon dating, see my book *What About Origins?* pages 127-136.)

In this method of dating it is assumed that the ratio of carbon-14 to "ordinary" carbon (i.e. carbon-12) in an organism when it died is the same as that which is measured in living plants and animals. This assumption would be correct *if* the earth is so old that the rate of production of carbon-14 in the upper atmosphere was balanced by its rate of disappearance from the biosphere—such an equilibrium will occur within 100,000 years depending upon the rate of production of radiocarbon. However, there is evidence to show that these two rates are *not* in equilibrium but that there is an imbalance between the rate of formation of carbon-14 and its rate of disappearance from the biosphere. Furthermore, in his book *Prehistory and Earth Models,* Professor Melvin Cook has shown (p.1 *ff*) that on the assumption that the neutron source strength and hence the rate of formation of carbon-14 is constant with time, this imbalance leads to the conclusion that the atmosphere is about 10,500 years old.

For those wishing to understand more clearly how Professor Cook arrives at this figure, let us consider the calculations involved. The maximum rate of formation of carbon-14 is calculated to be 2.94 atoms per square centimetre per second. Instead of using this figure, the intensity of the carbon-14 decay is used. Now 2.94 atoms/cm^2 sec corresponds to 20.8 counts/g min. To calculate the intensity at equilibrium, this figure has to be corrected for the ocean circulation lag and other factors, so the equilibrium intensity ($I_{equilibrium}$) is 21.3 counts/g min. The rate of disappearance of carbon-14 is 2.23 atoms/cm^2 sec. This figure has to be corrected by 5% for the entrance of carbon-14 into the biosphere via membrane diffusion to give 2.1 atoms/cm^2 sec. Hence the value of $I_{observed}$ is therefore 15.3 counts/g min.

The age of the atmosphere (t_a) is given by

$$1 - \frac{I_{observed}}{I_{equilibrium}} = e^{-\lambda t_a}$$

where $\lambda = 0.693/\tau$
and τ = the half-life of carbon-14 i.e. 5730 years.

A simple substitution and evaluation show that the age of the atmosphere (t_a) is 10,500 years. The error on the value of $I_{observed} / I_{equilibrium}$ is about $\pm$ 0.18. This gives an upper value of 26,800 years and a lower value of 7,600 years for the age of the atmosphere.

As stated previously, this age is calculated on the assumption that the rate of production of carbon-14 is a constant. There are, however, a number of factors that can influence this rate and because they may have varied in the past, then the rate of production of carbon-14 may also have varied and not have been constant. A faster rate of production will make the age of the atmosphere be younger than that calculated above, whereas a slower rate will make the atmosphere older than that calculated above.

The factors that can affect the rate of production of carbon-14 are:

(i)   *Cosmic Ray Intensity:* The greater the intensity of cosmic rays, the faster carbon-14 will be produced and *vice versa*.

(ii) *The Earth's Magnetic Field:* The earth's magnetic field deflects a large proportion of the incoming cosmic ray particles. There is evidence that the strength of this field has changed in the past, as we shall see. Any change in this field strength will affect the intensity of cosmic rays and hence the rate of production of carbon-14.

In passing, it should also be noted that magnetic field effects produced by the sun also influence the rate at which cosmic ray particles interact with the earth's atmosphere.

(iii) *The Amount of Water in the Atmosphere:* Not only will a magnetic field shield the earth from cosmic ray bombardment, but so will large amounts of water vapour. Interestingly from Genesis 2 vvs.5-6, it appears that the pre-flood world moisture requirements of plants were met by a subsoil water supply and heavy dew. Heavy dew implies an atmosphere nearly saturated with water vapour. The Bible also teaches that the pre-flood earth was surrounded by a water vapour canopy* (see Genesis 1 vvs.6-8) which would have inhibited the formation of carbon-14 because the atmosphere (and hence the nitrogen in it) would have been protected from cosmic ray bombardment. At the time of the flood, this

* Considerable criticisms have been made against the idea that the pre-flood earth had a water vapour canopy. The existence of this canopy has been rigorously defended by Joseph C Dillow in *The Waters Above* (Moody Press, 1979) parts of which were reproduced in the *Creation Research Society Quarterly* volume 15 (3) pp.148-159 (December 1978).

water vapour canopy collapsed (see Genesis 7 vvs.11-12) so the production of carbon-14 would have started because atmospheric nitrogen would no longer be protected from bombardment by cosmic rays. Hence the age of the atmosphere calculated above is really a determination of when the flood occurred.

Let us now turn our attention to yet another scientific discipline which also indicates that we are living on a young earth—that of studying the decay of the earth's di-polar magnetic field. This, in the opinion of many creationists, is one of the most important arguments that point positively to a young earth. This argument has been developed and highly refined by Dr Thomas G Barnes, Professor Emeritus of Physics at the University of Texas (El Paso). Dr Barnes' latest edition of his monograph *Origin and Destiny of the Earth's Magnetic Field* was published by the Institute for Creation Research in 1983. In his booklet *Science, Scripture and the Young Earth,* Dr Henry Morris has pointed out that the decay of the earth's magnetic field is a worldwide process, accurately measured for nearly 150 years (not just for a few years, as for radio-active decay processes). It is not subject to environmental changes since it is generated deep in the earth's interior. Furthermore, it is probably not subject to changes in decay rates, since the factors that control it cannot be affected by any outside conditions.

It is a known fact, though not well-publicised, that the earth's main magnetic field is decaying relatively rapidly. The values of the earth's magnetic moment M in amp metre^2 and the values of the equatorial magnetic field B_0 in tesla of the dipole from the period 1835 to 1965 are given in table 6. The earth's magnetic

Table 6 Magnetic Moment M and Equatorial
Magnetic Field B_0 of the Dipole, 1835 to
1965 (Earth radius $= 6.371 \times 10^6$ meter)

Scientists	Year (Epoch)	M (amp meter^2) $\times 10^{22}$	B_0 (tesla) $\times 10^{-5}$
Gauss	1835	8.558	3.309
Adams	1845	8.488	3.282
Adams	1880	8.363	3.234
Neumayer	1880	8.336	3.224
Fritsche	1885	8.347	3.228
Schmidt	1885	8.375	3.239
Vestine, *et al*	1905	8.291	3.206
Vestine, *et al*	1915	8.225	3.181
Dyson-Furner	1922	8.165	3.157
Vestine, *et al*	1925	8.149	3.151
Vestine, *et al*	1935	8.088	3.128
Jones-Melotte	1942.5	8.009	3.097
Vestine, *et al*	1945	8.065	3.119
Afanasieva	1945	8.010	3.097
U.S.C. & G.S.	1945	8.066	3.119
Fanselau-Kautzleben . .	1945	8.090	3.128
U.S.C. & G.S.	1955	8.035	3.107
Finch-Leaton	1955	8.067	3.120
Nagata-Oguti	1958.5	8.038	3.108
Cain, *et al*	1959	8.086	3.127
Fougere	1960	8.053	3.114
Adam, *et al*	1960	8.037	3.108
Jensen-Cain	1960	8.025	3.103
Leaton, *et al*	1965	8.013	3.099
Hurwitz, *et al*	1965	8.017	3.100

Taken from T G Barnes "Decay of the Earth's
Magnetic Moment and the Geochronological
Implications", *Creation Research Society Quarterly*
volume 8 (1) pp.24-29 (June 1971).

moment is due to circulating currents in the earth's core, which is thought to consist of a hot liquid metal, perhaps iron. These currents are extremely large and as there is no known mechanism to sustain these currents, the earth's magnetic moment is decaying.

Dr Barnes has shown that the magnetic moment of the earth is expected to decay exponentially because it is produced by real currents that dissipate energy through Joule heating. He concludes that the earth's magnetic moment is *not* produced by amperian currents (dissipationless currents) such as those that exist in permanently magnetised material. Dr Barnes has rejected permanently magnetised material as being the source of the earth's magnetic moment for two reasons:

(i) It would require greater intensity of magnetisation than has been observed in the crust of the earth, and

(ii) No magnetisation exists in the core material, because the high temperature there would destroy the magnetisation.

He then points out that the earth's magnetic moment being due to a system of circulating real currents will undoubtedly have associated, with its loops of current and its imperfect conductors, an inductance, L, and a resistance, R. Since there seems to be no dynamo or other energy source in the earth that can generate these currents, the current that does exist in the core must be decaying exponentially, as does any freely decaying current in a simple series circuit, in which the time to decay to e^{-1} of its initial value is equal to the ratio of the inductance, L, to the resistance, R. This means that the earth's magnetic moment will also be decaying exponentially.

When the values of the magnetic moment, M, in table 6 are plotted against time, t, on semi-log co-

Table 7   Value of the Magnetic Field at the
Surface of the Magnetic Equator for
Various Dates in the Past as Computed
from the 1,400 Year Half-Life Decay
Rate Currently Observed

Date	Magnetic Field (Tesla)
1965 A.D.	3.1×10^{-5}
1000 A.D.	5.0×10^{-5}
1 A.D.	8.3×10^{-5}
1000 B.C.	1.4×10^{-4}
2000 B.C.	2.3×10^{-4}
3000 B.C.	3.7×10^{-4}
4000 B.C.	6.1×10^{-4}
5000 B.C.	1.0×10^{-3}
6000 B.C.	1.7×10^{-3}
10,000 B.C.	1.2×10^{-2}
20,000 B.C.	1.8
30,000 B.C.	2.7×10^{2}
40,000 B.C.	4.0×10^{4}
50,000 B.C.	5.9×10^{6}
100,000 B.C.	4.2×10^{17}
200,000 B.C.	2×10^{39}
1,000,000 B.C.	3×10^{215}

Taken from Thomas G Barnes "Decay of the Earth's
Magnetic Moment and the Geochronological
Implications" *Creation Research Society Quarterly*,
volume 8 (1) pp.24-29 (June 1971).

ordinate paper, the points lie approximately on a straight line, as one would expect for an exponential decay of the earth's magnetic moment. This is also true for a plot of B_0 against t. The half-life of this decay is about 1,400 years. This means that in 1,400 years' time, the value of the earth's magnetic moment will be half its present value. It also means that 1,400 years ago, it was double its present value. Table 7 gives the equatorial value of the magnetic dipole field (main field) on the surface of the earth as a function of time.

Table 7 shows that if the earth was a million years old, then an *impossible* value of the strength of its magnetic field is reached. It also shows that if the earth were 20,000 years old, then when it was created the strength of its magnetic field on the surface of the earth would have been 18,000 gauss—stronger than the field between the pole pieces of the most powerful radar magnets. Dr Barnes has pointed out that it is not very plausible that the core of the earth could have stayed together with the Joule heat that would have been associated with the currents producing such a strong field. From this, Dr Barnes concludes that the origin of the earth's magnetic moment, and hence the earth, is much less than 20,000 years ago.

The evolutionist, of course, does not accept that the earth's magnetic field is decaying exponentially and the associated conclusion that the earth must be less than 20,000 years old. Instead, he believes in the dynamo hypothesis—that there is in the molten core of the earth a dynamo which generates the electric currents required to power the earth's magnetic field for more than four and a half thousand million years. Firstly, it should be realised that there is no known mechanism for generating the electric current in the dynamo hypothesis, and secondly, there is no real evidence that a dynamo even exists. In fact, the only real basis for this hypothesis is that it avoids the young earth implications of the electrical current theory which Dr Thomas Barnes shows to be strongly supported by all known data and by sound physics.

The evolutionist also argues that the earth's magnetic field has gone through many reversals, changing its polarity from north to south and back again many times at irregular intervals. There is not space here to deal with the arguments and counter arguments about this. Those wishing to know these in detail are advised to read the second revised and expanded edition of Dr Thomas Barnes' *Origin and Destiny of the Earth's Magnetic Field*. Suffice it to say that "There are innumerable local magnetic fields which can strongly influence and affect measurements in any given region. Thus to think that the remanent magnetism in a suite of rocks or an archæological site could be used to determine the earth's overall dipole magnetic strength or direction at that time in history is naive extrapolation carried to extremes" (Dr Henry Morris, *Science, Scripture and the Young Earth*, p.28).

An editorial in that prestigious journal *Science* on 8 January 1982 stated that "Those who propound creationism...have no substantial body of experimental data to back their prejudices." This is not so! As we have seen in this chapter, there is evidence from a variety of scientific disciplines to show that far from being thousands of millions of years old, the earth is only a few thousand years old. Table 8 summarises this evidence, all of which indicates that the earth is less than 20,000 years old. It is the evolutionist with his anti-God 'chance-alone-can-do-it-all-given-enough-time' ideas that is prejudiced, for he knows that if he accepts that the earth is less than 20,000 years old, then there has not been enough time for his

Table 8 Summary of the Scientific Evidence for a Young Earth

Method	Age of the Earth	Assumptions
A Life-time of short-period comets.	Less than 10,000 years.	(i) No short-period comets supplied to the solar system from time to time. (ii) Observed rate of disintegration of short-period comets unaltered during the last 10,000 years.
B Amount of micrometeoric dust settling onto the earth's surface.	9,000—26,000 years.	(i) Micrometeoric dust being transported by the rivers into the oceans. (ii) Observed rate of influx of micrometeoric dust onto the earth's surface fairly constant. (iii) No nickel in the oceans to start with.
C Amount of helium-4 in the atmosphere.	About 11,000 years.	(i) Observed rate of efflux of helium-4 into the atmosphere constant during the last 11,000 years. (ii) No helium-4 in the atmosphere to begin with.
D Imbalance of the rate of formation of radiocarbon in the atmosphere and its rate of disappearance from the biosphere.	About 10,500 years (for the the atmosphere).	(i) Rate of production of carbon-14 is a constant. (ii) No carbon-14 in the atmosphere to begin with.
E Decay of the earth's magnetic field.	Less than 20,000 years.	(i) The earth's magnetic field is due to a magnetic dipole which is decaying exponentially.

chance-alone processes to have brought about the world in which we live. He would have to abandon his cherished ideas and acknowledge the existence of a Creator, with all the consequences of this acknowledgement.

11.
A Light Problem?

We saw in the last chapter that there is evidence from a variety of scientific disciplines to show that the earth and the solar system are less than 20,000 years old. As the majority of creationists maintain that this is also the age of the universe, there appears to be what is often called "a light problem". This may be summarised as follows: if we accept the current description of the universe explained to us by astronomers, then there are *many* stars within our own galaxy (the Milky Way) as well as *all* the stars in all the other galaxies in the universe which are more than 20,000 light years away i.e. the distance is further than light can travel (at 186,000 miles per second) in 20,000 years. Hence if the universe is only 20,000 years old, the problem is: how is it possible to see a star which is further than 20,000 light years, for it will take longer than 20,000 years for the light to travel from that star to the earth.

A number of solutions to this problem have been put forward by creationists, and I want us to consider these in turn. The first solution is to maintain that the light from the stars was created instantaneously in rays throughout space at the same time that the stars were created. This would mean that light now arriving upon the earth, appearing to come from a particular star more than 20,000 light years away, would not actually be coming from that star at all.

The light rays would have been created *in situ* and so any indication of the occurrence of past historical events (e.g. changes in brightness) would not be real historical events at all, but the light rays would contain the information to make it appear to us that these events occurred.

Many creationists find this simple explanation logically unacceptable even though there is no reason why God could not have created the universe in this way. I realise that many non-Christian scientists would not accept such an explanation, arguing that it would make the study of the history of stars meaningless. Theologically, it can be argued that if God has created the universe in this way, then He has *not* deceived mankind, for He has given us His Word to tell us that He created the universe recently.

Another solution to overcoming the light problem is to accept the "extended period" interpretation of the early verses of Genesis chapter one. This interpretation insists that a very long time period elapsed between the original creation of "the heavens and the earth" in verse 1 and the creation of light on earth in verse 3. During this time, it is argued that the earth existed but was "without form" (featureless?) and "void" (empty of life?). Professor Edgar Andrews in his book *God, Science and Evolution* comments on this particular interpretation as follows (p.79):

> "This 'extended period' interpretation of Genesis 1:2 can provide a partial recon-ciliation with geological time in that it affords time for the earth to be formed from interstellar material by natural process and could also account for the radiometric ages of igneous and non-fossiliferous metamorphic and sediment-ary rocks. It does not, however, permit the

great ages attributed to the fossil record
nor sufficient time for the natural
evolution of life and the biosphere."

This interpretation appears to be theologically
unsound on two scores. The first is that there does not
appear to be room for such an interpretation in view
of the length and meaning of the creation days in
Genesis chapter one—for a detailed discussion see
chapter 3. The second biblical difficulty is the
statement found in the fourth commandment: "For
in six days the Lord made heaven and earth, the sea,
and all that in them is..."(Exodus 20 v.11, AV).
The verse does not permit such an "extended period"
interpretation of Genesis chapter one. Furthermore,
it does also seem inconceivable that God created the
heavens and the earth ("lighted the blue touch-
paper" so to speak) and then a few thousand million
years later came and created things on the earth as
recorded in Genesis 1 vvs.3 onwards in six successive
days!

Three different scientific solutions have been
proposed by creationists to answer the light problem.
The first concerns the very real fact that distances in
space cannot be accurately measured and so the
universe may be less than 20,000 light years in radius.
Distances to various astronomical bodies (e.g. planets
and stars) are calculated using various methods. Stars
which are "near" (i.e. up to 200 light years away) are
measured using the method of triangulation or
parallax. This method is employed by surveyors
using the well-known law of trigonometry that if you
know the base and two angles of a triangle, it is
possible to calculate its height. In practice what
happens is that as the earth moves in its orbit around
the sun, the nearer stars (i.e. those up to 200 light
years away) appear to move against the background

of the very distant "fixed" stars. This apparent movement is called parallax and it is this angular movement that is measured as the earth moves in six months from one side of its orbit around the sun to the other. Knowing that the base of the triangle is twice the distance of the earth to the sun (about 186 million miles) and the angular movement, it is possible to calculate the distance to the star.

The limitations of this method should be obvious. Because distances to the stars are so great, the sides of the triangle are almost perpendicular and so the angular movement of any particular star is extremely small. If we scale things down, we may get an idea of the problem. Let us suppose that the distance from the earth to the sun is 8 cm. On this scale, the nearest star would be nearly 24 km away! So we have a triangle with the base 8 cm long and the perpendicular 24 km long. Hence the angular movement of the star would have to be measured in just a few seconds of arc (a second of arc is one sixtieth of a minute of arc which in turn is a sixtieth of a degree).

The distances to stars which are so far away that their distances cannot be measured by this method of parallax because they appear to be "fixed", are determined by their presumed sizes and intensities. The distances to galaxies are calculated by their so-called red shift. When light coming from these galaxies is studied spectroscopically, the emission or absorption lines of the elements are not seen at their usual wave length but are shifted toward the red end of the spectrum. It is believed that the greater the red shift, the greater the distance to the galaxy. However, the red shift distance scale is based upon the foundation of the so-called Cepheid variable distance scale, which itself has a considerable degree of possible error for it is based on unproven and unprovable assumptions. Hence red shift may have nothing at all to do with distance and so the universe may not be as huge as astronomers believe it to be. It must be pointed out, however, that very few astronomers would concede that the universe could be less than 20,000 light years' radius.

The second scientific explanation, which is the one most favoured by creationists, is that light takes what may be called a "short-cut" as it travels through space. This is difficult to visualise but suffice it to say that there are two concepts of the "shape" of outer space. One is that it is straight-line (Euclidean) and the other that it is curved (Riemannian). Now, based on observations of twenty-seven binary star systems, it has been proposed that light in deep space does in fact travel in curved paths on Riemannian surfaces (P Moon and D E Spencer "Binary Stars and the Velocity of Light", *Journal of the Optical Society of America*, volume 43 pp.635-641, August 1953). Evidence was also adduced that the radius of curvature of space is five light years.

Now the formula for converting straight-line space to curved space is:

$$s = 2R \tan^{-1}(r / 2R)$$

where s = the distance in Riemannian space,
r = the distance in Euclidean space,
and R = the radius of curvature of the curved space.

Using this formula and a radius of curvature of five light years, the time for light to reach us from points

Table 9   Euclidean and Riemannian Distances

Euclidean Distance in Light Years	Riemannian Distance in Actual Time
1	0.997 years
4	3.81
10	7.85
30	12.5
100	14.7
1,000	15.6
10,000	15.7
Infinite	15.71

Taken from table V of "Binary Stars and the Velocity of Light" by P Moon and D E Spencer published in *Journal of the Optical Society of America* volume 43 pp.635-641 (August 1953).

within our own solar system is practically the same for either Euclidean or Riemannian distances. There is not much of a change even out to the nearest star at just over four light years away (see table 9). However, if we insert an infinite Euclidean distance for the farthest conceivable star, it would take only 15.71 years for the light to reach us from that distance. Hence the idea of light travelling in curved space effectively eliminates the problem of seeing stars at Euclidean distances greater than 20,000 light years, if the universe is only 20,000 years old. The light gets here sooner not because its velocity has increased but because the effective distance that it travels is smaller.

The third and last scientific solution to the light problem that I want us to consider is the one that maintains that the speed of light was considerably faster in the past and that it has slowed down to its present value. Hence light from distant objects would have got here sooner than present rates indicate. The Australian scientist Barry Setterfield has shown that there is evidence that light was travelling much faster in the past and that its speed decreased rapidly at first and then more gradually until it reached a constant level in 1960. Between 1675 and 1976, there were fifty-two experimental determinations of the value of the speed of light—see table 10. These values are *not* constant but become progressively lower until they taper off to a constant in 1960. In fact, there is a drop in value of over 1500 km/sec in the 285 year period 1675 to 1960.

To find a scientific explanation for these observations of the apparent anomaly in the value of the speed of light, Barry Setterfield programmed a computer to search for the best curve to fit the data. This turned out to be a curve with the equation

$$c = A \operatorname{cosec}^2 (KT)$$
where c = speed of light
T = time
and A and K are constants.
(The r^2 value of the fit was 0.998.)

One consequence of this is that the time when the speed of light started to slow down is 4082 ± 100 BC and the other is that light could have reached us from the farthest point of the universe in less than 6,000 years.

There are other consequences of Barry Setterfield's work. These are discussed in detail in *The Velocity of*

Table 10 Experimental determinations of the speed of light

Experimenter	Date	Observed Value Km/sec	
Roemer	1675.0	301,300	± 200
Bradley	1728.0	301,000	
Cornu	1871.0	300,400	± 200
Cornu-Helmert	1874.8	299,990	
Michelson	1879.5	299,910	± 50
Newcombe	1882.7	299,860	± 30
Michelson	1882.8	299,853	± 60
	1885.0	299,940	
Perrotin	1902.4	299,901	± 84
Perrotin	1902.8	299,895	
Perrotin	1906.0	299,880	
Michelson	1924.0	299,802	± 30
Michelson	1926.5	299,796	± 4
Mittelstaedt	1928.0	299,778	± 10
Pease-Pearson	1932.5	299,774	± 11
Anderson	1939.0	299,771	± 12
Huttel	1940.0	299,768	± 10
Essen	1947.0	299,797	± 3
Aslakson	1949.0	299,792.4	± 5.5
Bergstrand	1949.0	299,796	± 2
Essen	1950.0	299,792.5	± 1
Bergstrand	1950.0	299,793.1	± 1
Bergstrand	1951.0	299,793.1	± 2.5
Aslakson	1951.0	299,794.2	± 1.4
Froome	1951.0	299,792.6	± 1.3
Kraus	1953.0	299,800	
Froome	1954.0	299,792.75	± 0.35
Florman	1954.0	299,795.1	± 3.1

Table 10 continued

Experimenter	Date	Observed Value Km/sec	
Scholdstrom	1955.0	299,792.4	± 0.4
Plyler, Blaine & Cannon	1955.0	299,792.0	± 6
Plyler *et al*	1955.0	299,793.0	
Cohen *et al*	1955.0	299,793.0	± 0.3
Bergstrand	1956.0	299,793.0	± 0.3
Wadley	1956.0	299,792.9	± 2
Rank, Bennett & Bennet	1956.0	299,791.9	± 2
Edge	1956.0	299,792.4	± 0.4
Wadley	1957.0	299,792.6	± 1.2
Bergstrand	1957.0	299,792.9	± 0.2
Rank *et al*	1957.0	299,793.7	± 0.7
Rank *et al*	1957.0	299,793.2	
Mulligan & McDonald	1957.0	299,792.8	± 0.6
Froome	1958.0	299,792.5	± 0.1
Corson & Lorraine	1962.0	299,790	
Karolus	1966.0	299,792.1	± 1
Helmberger	1966	299,792.44	± 0.2
Simkin *et al*	1967.0	299,792.56	± 0.11
ITT Staff	1970.0	299,793	
Bay, Luther & White	1972.0	299,792.462	± 0.018
Evenson	1973.0	299,792.4574	± 0.0011
Blaney	1974.0	299,792.4590	± 0.0008
CCDM (France)	1975.0	299,792.458	± 0.004
	1976.0	299,792.456	

Taken from table 3 on page 13 of *The Velocity of Light and the Age of the Universe* by Barry Setterfield.

Light and the Age of the Universe by Barry Setterfield and
they include changes in the rates of decay of radio-
active isotopes and the fact that some well-known
physical constants such as Planck's constant may not
have been constant with time at all. These factors,
and others which Setterfield discusses, may have a
considerable bearing upon the nature of the universe
as we understand it.

In this chapter, we have considered various
solutions to the problem of seeing stars which are so
far away that it would take light, travelling at its
present measured rate, longer to travel the distance
from the star to the earth than the 20,000 year age of
the universe believed by many creationists. The idea
of God creating light rays *in situ* when He created the
stars would mean that we would observe events that
never actually took place. Those who reject this idea
(and I do for one), do so on philosophical grounds
arguing that they find it logically unacceptable. We
then saw that the "extended period" interpretation
of the early verses of Genesis chapter one is
theologically unacceptable and does not seem to
make sense scientifically.

Turning to the scientific explanations, it seems
unlikely that the universe is as small as 20,000 light
years in radius. Either one of the last two scientific
explanations seems to be the most likely explanation
of why we are able to see very distant stars if we are
living in a young universe. As I stated when we
considered it, the majority of creationists accept the
curved space explanation to the light problem.
Although the idea of light slowing down is not new,
Barry Setterfield has produced some experimental
evidence to show this has occurred in recent history
and he has rigorously applied his findings to other
branches of physics.

I purposely put a question mark after the title of this chapter for I do not believe that there is a light problem at all. As we have seen there are a number of sound explanations for how it is possible to see stars which are more than 20,000 light years away, if the universe is less than 20,000 years old — an age which, as we have seen, is adduced from a variety of scientific disciplines.

12.
Conclusion

In this section we have looked at the problem of determining the age of the earth without using the written record contained in the early chapters of Genesis. First of all we considered how rocks are dated, and we saw that this was done by the use of index fossils. We saw that the age of the index fossil is based on its supposed evolution, and the proof of evolution is the age of the rocks in which the fossils are found. Because of such circular reasoning, fossils cannot provide a satisfactory method of dating rocks.

When we turned our attention to radiometric dating, we saw that this relies heavily upon assumptions about which there is no proof whether or not they are correct. We also looked at some of the problems encountered in attempting to obtain a date for a rock and considered some of the discordant dates obtained using different radiometric methods.

We then spent a lot of time looking at the scientific evidence for a young earth, carefully noting the assumptions made in each of the methods employed to determine the age of the earth. We saw that this evidence indicates that the age of the earth should be measured in thousands rather than thousands of millions of years.

We then considered the apparent problem of how it is possible to see stars which are further than 20,000 light years away if the universe is only 20,000 years old. We saw that there are various solutions to this problem: the most favoured solution up to now being that light travels in Riemannian space and so takes a "short-cut". We also considered the experimental evidence that light has been slowing down in the recent past.

Now, we must consider all things...

PART THREE

All Things Considered

13.
General Conclusion

We set out to try to discover the answer to the question "How old is the earth?" I think that by now you must be aware that a very definite and accurate age cannot be given as an answer to this question for neither the Bible nor science is able to give the actual date when the earth came into being. There are, however, very definite limits to the age of the earth.

From biblical considerations, we concluded that Adam and Eve were created when the earth was a mere six days old. We know that these days are literal days—they are not be be confused with geological periods or indeed with 1000 year periods of time. We also know that there cannot be any time period or gap between Genesis 1 v.1 and 1 v.2. When we considered the genealogies in Genesis chapters five and eleven, we had to conclude that it is impossible to construct a chronology from them and so arrive at a date for the creation of Adam. However, we saw that there are limits to how far the genealogies in Genesis chapters five and eleven can be stretched before they become meaningless. Indeed, if Adam had been created about 100,000 BC then such a position would be reached.

When we turned to scientific considerations, we saw that geologists tend to date rocks by means of so-called index fossils. Such rocks are dated by a process

of circular reasoning: the age of a fossil is determined
by the theory of evolution, which in turn relies for its
support and proof on the age of the rock in which the
fossil is found. When we turned our attention to
radiometric dating, we saw that this relies heavily
upon assumptions about which there is no proof
whether or not they are correct. We then considered
some of the problems encountered when trying to
date rocks using radiometric dating techniques and
looked at some of the peculiar results obtained.

We also examined some of the scientific data that
indicate that the earth is thousands rather than
thousands of millions of years old. Totally different
methods gave consistent indications that the earth is
less than 20,000 years old. The significance of this
figure is that it is consistent with the age of the earth
that is indicated from a study of the early chapters of
the Bible. We must not forget that these various
methods might have indicated that we live on an
earth which is about 20 *million* years old, and this
would have been inconsistent with Scripture. But
these methods do not suggest such an age. Instead,
they suggest an age which is *consistent* with the clear
teaching of Scripture. Thus, once again, there is
harmony between the Bible and science.

We then considered the apparent problem of how
it is possible to see stars which are further than 20,000
light years away if the universe is only 20,000 years
old. For light, travelling at its present rate, would
take longer than 20,000 years to travel the distance
from those stars to the earth. We considered various
solutions to this problem. The idea of God creating
light rays *in situ* when He created the stars was one
explanation which some find philosophically unacceptable. The "extended period" interpretation of
the early verses of Genesis chapter one is theologically

unacceptable. It seems unlikely that the universe is as small as 20,000 light years radius. Although the majority of creationists overcome the so-called light problem by accepting that light travels in Riemannian space and so takes a "short-cut", as it were, there appears to be experimental evidence that light has been slowing down in the recent past and so this might be the solution to the light problem.

Before we began our biblical and scientific considerations of the age of the earth, however, we considered the effect the answer to this question would have on the theory of evolution. Clearly, if this earth is less than 20,000 years old, then there has been *no time* for evolution! This means that we are left with the alternative to evolution as an explanation of life on earth — that of creation. Now the fact that the age indicated from scientific considerations is consistent with that taught by the Bible further strengthens the idea of creation as an explanation of origins. However, as I have emphasised in my booklet *The Scientific Case for Creation*, although science can point you in the direction of believing in creation, science *cannot* tell you who the Creator is and how we can have a very special relationship with Him. We have to turn to the Bible to find out the answers to these questions.

The Bible teaches that the Creator is God—the Lord God Almighty. He is the One who created all things and nothing would exist if it were not for Him. We read in Genesis chapter one that God created man in His own image and from Genesis chapter two we can see that God and Adam had a very special relationship with each other. This relationship was, however, marred when Adam, of his own free will, disobeyed God's explicit command to him. In other words, Adam sinned by disobeying God's command.

This is what sin is—disobeying God's commands. Because Adam sinned, we all sin— there is no-one who can say that he has never sinned. And it is *sin* that separates created man from his Creator. Now the question is: how can this sin problem be resolved so that men and women can have a special relationship with God, as Adam did in the garden of Eden? How can you get rid of your sin so that you can know God?

The answer to the sin problem is found in Jesus Christ, God's only begotten Son. In fact, the Bible tells us that even before the creation of the world, the plan of salvation was known to God. He had decided that the only way for sinful human beings to be right with God was for them to have their sins washed away in the blood of the Lord Jesus Christ, God's only begotten Son:

> "For you know that it was not with perishable things such as silver or gold that you were redeemed from the empty way of life handed down to you from your forefathers, but with the precious blood of Christ, a lamb without blemish or defect. He was chosen before the creation of the world, but was revealed in these last times for your sake."
>
> 1 Peter 1 vvs. 18-20 (NIV)

In Revelation 13 v.8, Jesus Christ is again pictured as a lamb "that was slain from the creation of the world" (NIV).

The Bible is quite explicit about the fact that if you do not recognise sin in your life, and if you do not turn with true repentance to God and be washed clean in the blood of the Lamb of God, (i.e. the Lord Jesus Christ) and be clothed with the garment of His righteousness, then you are at enmity with God. It is God's desire for His creatures to repent and believe the gospel — the good news about having your sins washed away in the blood that was shed on Calvary's cross.

Interestingly, the Bible also teaches that those that repent and have their sins forgiven them and are redeemed by the blood of the Lamb of God were chosen by God to do so before the creation of the world:

> "For he chose us in him before the creation of the world to be holy and blameless in his sight. In love he predestined us to be adopted as his sons through Jesus Christ, in accordance with his pleasure and will—to the praise of his glorious grace, which he has freely given us in the One he loves. In him we have redemption through his blood, the forgiveness of sins, in accordance with the riches of God's grace that he lavished on us with all wisdom and understanding."
>
> Ephesians 1 vvs.4-8 (NIV)

And their names were written in the book of life from the creation of the world (Revelation 17 v.8). Although this doctrine of predestination is clearly taught in Scripture, the responsibility is upon each one of us to repent of our sins and believe on the Lord Jesus Christ for our redemption in and through the blood which He shed on that cruel cross on Calvary.

Another fact which we learn from Scripture is that the earth will not last for ever. A long time ago, the Lord promised Noah that He would not destroy the earth again with a flood. (See Genesis 9 vvs.8-17.) However, the Bible teaches that one day, not only the earth, but the entire universe will be destroyed *by fire:*

> "But the day of the Lord will come like a thief. The heavens will disappear with a

roar; the elements will be destroyed by fire,
and the earth and everything in it will be
burned up (margin).
That day will bring about the destruction
of the heavens by fire, and the elements
will melt in the heat."

2 Peter 3 vvs.10 and 12 (NIV)

Peter goes on to say in verse 13 that "We are looking
forward to a new heaven and a new earth, the home
of righteousness," and this is what the Apostle John
saw in a vision which is recorded for us in Revelation
21 v.1 (NIV):

"Then I saw a new heaven and a new
earth, for the first heaven and the first
earth had passed away."

We also learn from the book of Revelation that
those whose names are not written in the book of life
do not get to see and enjoy the new heaven and the
new earth where there is perfect peace and perfect
fellowship with God. Instead, those that have not
repented of their sins, those that have not been
washed in the blood of the Lamb of God are thrown
into the lake of fire (usually called "hell") and are
tormented day and night for ever and ever. The day
of judgement is a fearful day and none will escape it.
What will the Son of God say to you on that day? Will
He say: "Come you who are blessed by my Father,
take your inheritance, the kingdom prepared for you
since the creation of the world."? Or will He say: "I
never knew you: depart from me, ye that work
iniquity"?

Before we finally conclude our study of the age of
the earth, I want us to return to the concept of the
superficial appearance of age—something we looked
at in chapter 5 at the end of our Biblical
considerations. This concept can have a significant

effect on attempts to arrive at the age of the earth for, though created in an instant, at that very moment the earth could have appeared to be hundreds or even thousands of years old! To appreciate this, let us consider the soil in the garden of Eden. The soil scientist K Mickey in *Man and the Soil* (International Harvester Co, 1945) informs us on page 17 that "The rate at which nature builds soil under the most favourable conditions has been estimated all the way from 300 to 1000 years for a single inch." Hence the soil in the garden of Eden would have had a superficial appearance of age. Assuming the soil was six inches deep, its "age" could be calculated to be between 1800 and 6000 years—even though in reality it was only a few days old.

This type of argument has been used effectively by R G Korthals in an article called "There Was Evening—And There Was Morning" published in *Scientific Studies in Special Creation* (Presbyterian & Reformed, 1971). The superficial appearance of age of the newly created world is illustrated as follows:

> "And now let us imagine that Adam was a scientist interested in determining the age of the earth. He starts his research on the 8th day after creation, in and around the garden of Eden. He looks at himself and Eve, and, realising that they are both mature individuals, states that they and the earth are at least 20 years old. He cuts down a tree in order to build a fire, and counts the growth rings. According to this, the earth is at least 139 years old. He and Eve stroll down to the river banks, where he notices the deep channel cut by the stream. By carefully measuring the erosion rate, he estimates and concludes that 5,000

years have gone by since the stream started
as a tiny trickle. They pause and marvel at
the magnificent mountains in the distance,
watching the sun as it slowly sinks beneath
the peaks. He knows that internal
pressures within the earth are slowly
pushing these mountains higher—and,
using the present established rate, he
calculates that the mountain range is at
least 1.5 billion years old. The next day
they explore a canyon started 750,000
years ago by a river and marvel at the
layers of rock, some formed almost 3
billion years in the past, according to his
geologic time scale, which is based upon
rock formation phenomena...And so
Adam, the scientist, determines the age of
the world upon which he is living—a
world which according to his reasoning,
observations, calculations and assumptions, is at least 3 billion years old—yet it is
a world which was created just 8 days
earlier."

Some object to this doctrine of superficial
appearance of age, arguing that it makes God a
deceiver of men. God, however, has *not* deceived
us—He has given us His Word, the Bible, to tell us
what He has done, and as A E Carnell has pointed out
(quoted by Professor J C Whitcomb in *The Early Earth*
on page 37):

"We must cheerfully admit God's moral
right to create things which only appear,
but are not actually, old. The limits of how
God has employed this privilege must be
measured—in the last analysis—not from
science, but from Scripture."

We therefore have only ourselves to blame if we reject the written Word of God. The attitude of those who do reject it, however, only indicates that they are at enmity with their Creator. If you are in such a position, I would encourage you to read this chapter again and to reconsider God's love for you and I would implore you to repent of your sins and be washed clean in the blood of the Lord Jesus Christ, God's only begotten Son, who was chosen before the creation of the world to be mankind's redeemer.

Appendix – Bibliography

Clues to Creation in Genesis by P J Wiseman (Marshall, Morgan & Scott, 1977).

Critique of Radiometric Dating by H S Slusher (Institute for Creation Research, El Cajon, California, 1973).

Geological Time by J F Kirkaldy (Oliver & Boyd, Edinburgh, 1971).

God, Science & Evolution by E H Andrews (Evangelical Press, 1980).

Historical and Chronological Charts prepared by J C Whitcomb (Grace Theological Seminary):
   No. 1 From the Creation to Abraham.
   No. 2 Chart of Old Testament Patriarchs and Judges.

Origin and Destiny of the Earth's Magnetic Field by T G Barnes (Institute for Creation Research, El Cajon, 1983). Second Edition.

Prehistory and Earth Models by M A Cook (Max Parrish, London, 1966).

Science, Scripture & the Young Earth by H M Morris (Institute for Creation Research, El Cajon, 1983).

Scientific Creationism edited by H M Morris (Creation-Life Publishers, 1974).

The Age of the Solar System by H S Slusher and S J Duursma (Institute for Creation Research, El Cajon, 1978).

The Early Earth by J C Whitcomb (Evangelical Press, 1972).

The Earth, the Stars and the Bible by P M Steidl (Presbyterian & Reformed, 1979).

The Genesis Flood by H M Morris and J C Whitcomb (Presbyterian & Reformed, 1961).

The Scientific Case for Creation by A J Monty White (Heath Christian Trust, Cardiff, 1984).

The Velocity of Light and the Age of the Universe by B Setterfield (Creation Science Association, Adelaide, Australia, 1983).

Unformed and Unfilled by W W Fields (Presbyterian & Reformed, 1976).

What About Origins? by A J Monty White (Dunestone Printers Ltd, 1978).